THE KING OF
SCHNORRERS

THE KING OF SCHNORRERS

Israel Zangwill

Introduction to the Dover Edition by
MAURICE WOHLGELERNTER

DOVER PUBLICATIONS, INC.
Mineola, New York

Bibliographical Note

This Dover edition, first published in 2003, is an unabridged republication of the 1965 Dover reprint which consisted of the text as published in 1864 by William Heinemann, London, and a new Introduction by Maurice Wohlgelernter that was specially prepared for the Dover edition.

Library of Congress Cataloging-in-Publication Data

Zangwill, Israel, 1864-1926.
    The king of Schnorrers / Israel Zangwill ; with a new introduction by Maurice Wohlgelernter.
      p. cm.
   ISBN 0-486-42872-9 (pbk.)
    1. Jews—England—Fiction. 2. London (England)—Fiction. I. Title.

PR5922 .K5 2003
823'.8—dc21
                                            2002192221

Manufactured in the United States of America
Dover Publications, Inc., 31 East 2nd Street, Mineola, N.Y. 11501

INTRODUCTION TO THE DOVER EDITION

Central to the life and thought of Israel Zangwill was the ghetto. Born in London's East End on January 21, 1864, the son of a peddler, he grew up in the "Judea, a cosmos in little" of that English metropolis. Among its motley inhabitants living off one another, he reminds us, there were "prize-fighters and scientists, philosophers and 'fences,' gymnasts and money lenders, scholars and stock-brokers, philosophers, musicians, chess players, poets, comics, singers, saints, publicans, politicians, warriors, poltroons, mathematicians, actors, foreign correspondents,"[1] and, of course, the ubiquitous *schnorrer*. Nearly all of these, in one guise or another, fill the pages of Zangwill's works. The last figure, his professionally importuning beggar, makes his most notable appearance in *The King of Schnorrers*.

Anxious to penetrate beyond the ghetto and to avoid becoming an itinerant peddler like his father, who, traveling about the countryside, was "shamelessly despoiled . . . of his merchandise, or bullied and blustered out . . . of his fair price"[2] or sent bleeding to bed by rowdies, Zangwill determined early to better his lot. While serving as student-teacher at Jews Free School, he enrolled at the University of London, where, after assiduously attending to his studies, he was awarded an honors degree in literature in 1884.

Thus, educated as a Jew and an Englishman, Zangwill attempted and in great measure succeeded in integrating in his life and works the best of both worlds and later in offering them to his readers who found him enlightening and piquant at the same time. As one critic has observed, "In his dual striving to

[1] Israel Zangwill, *Children of the Ghetto* (New York, 1898), p. xv.
[2] *Ibid.*, p. 66.

extend universally the boundaries of both the ideas that he loved, the Jewish and the English, Zangwill was, as truly as Blake, struggling to build Jerusalem in England's 'green and pleasant land.' "[3] If the melting of these two ideas into a common spirit was substantially achieved in England after having been boiled in the pot of hope and despair for some seven centuries, much of the credit must be granted to Zangwill.

In addition, Zangwill was also a novelist, playwright, poet, essayist, Zionist, Territorialist, pacifist, polemicist, suffragist and member of other sundry quasi-political movements. That he expended so much energy on organizations only remotely connected with his fictional art is not surprising when we stop to consider that he was a product of the emancipation. Zangwill's catholic interests can best be appreciated if they are placed against the background of the nineteenth century, when the West-European Jew, granted the rights and privileges of citizenship, proceeded to merge his interests with those of his neighbors to insure the new spirit of justice, brotherhood and liberty that had arisen in the world.

And the quest for freedom manifested itself early in Zangwill's career. Believing strongly in his fundamental right to a free and unfettered life, Zangwill resigned his instructorship at Jews Free School for reasons which, though never fully explained, would appear to have dealt with freedom of speech. Losing his only source of income, but apparently confident of his ability, Zangwill, in 1884, decided to become a writer. And once he began to write, he could not stop. A torrent of books fell from his pen.

II

The main body of Zangwill's work may be divided into two broad categories: Jewish and non-Jewish. The works in the latter category, though not as successful as those dealing with ghetto themes, are nevertheless formidable. Beginning with the pseudonymous novel *The Premier and the Painter* (1888), written in collaboration with his friend Louis Cowen, Zangwill wrote among other things: *The Celibates' Club* (1891), *The Master*

[3] Joseph Leftwich, *Israel Zangwill* (New York, 1957), p. 47.

(1894), *Without Prejudice* (1896), *The Mantle of Elijah* (1900), *The Grey Wig* (1903), *Italian Fantasies* (1910), *The War God* (1911), *The Next Religion* (1912), *Plaster Saints* (1915), *The War for the World* (1916), *Chosen Peoples* (1917), *Too Much Money* (1918), *The Principle of Nationalities* (1918), *Jinny the Carrier* (1919), *The Cockpit* (1921), *The Forcing House* (1922) and *We Moderns* (1924).

Among the ghetto works we find, first, his most famous novel *Children of the Ghetto* (1892), then *Ghetto Tragedies* (1893), *Dreamers of the Ghetto* (1898), *Blind Children* (1903), *Ghetto Comedies* (1907), *The Melting Pot* (1908), *The Voice of Jerusalem* (1921), translations from the *Selected Religious Poems of Solomon Ibn Gabirol* (1923) and the posthumous collection of *Speeches, Articles and Letters* (1937). He also contributed countless articles, letters, poems and speeches, as yet uncollected, that appeared in dailies, weeklies, monthlies and quarterlies the world over.

Among the second group, the phenomenally well-received *The King of Schnorrers* (1894), a comic tale of a typical Jewish beggar in an eighteenth-century setting, at once set a great part of London laughing. For all its spontaneous drollery, it has a conscientiously constructed historical background. Disregarding the crude definition, often put, that comedy must have a happy ending, Zangwill very carefully attempted, like the other humorists who gathered about Jerome K. Jerome's *The Idler* in which, incidentally, this work first appeared serially, to invest his characters, especially the *Schnorrer,* with the double mask of tragedy and comedy.

Zangwill, asserting in *Ghetto Comedies* that "Jewish life is always tragi-comedy," was convinced that the comic spirit, which, like the tragic, always existed in the gloomy alleys of the ghetto, abetted the unconquerable faith that sustained his people in their struggle for survival. For, paradoxically, the comic spirit derived from a background of sorrow and evil and the need to accept them. Tragedy and comedy were, in fact, complementary aspects of ghetto life.

To be sure, Zangwill often uses the term "humor" instead of comedy when he wishes to civilize the ghetto inhabitants by alluding to the quality of their intellect. But, though "comedy" and "humor" are admittedly different in form, their ultimate interest, according to Zangwill, is the same. Both are interested in the influence of the social world upon the characters of men. Both are less concerned with beginnings or endings or surroundings than with what men are now doing. Both, in fact, laugh through the mind. Moreover, both contain a philosophic attitude that says, "whenever a man laughs humorously there is an element which, if his sensitivity were sufficiently exaggerated, would contain the possibility of tears. He is a man who has suffered or failed of something. And although in the humor of art he usually arrives at something else, in the humor of everyday life he frequently arrives at nothing at all."[4] Since the children of the ghetto arrived nowhere at all, humor became for them, Zangwill believed, an adroit and exquisite device by which their nerves outwitted the stings and paltry bitternesses of life.

And where but in the ghetto were the stings and bitternesses of life more manifest? There, amid the squalor of slum alleys, in order to mollify their tragic existence, human beings would, at times, wax out of proportion, become overblown, pretentious, hypocritical, pedantic and fantastically delicate. Mined with conceit, they would appear falsely humble. Occasionally, they would even violate the unwritten but perceptible laws binding them in consideration to each other, offending reason and justice. Precisely at such times, the "comic spirit," appearing overhead, would humanely malign them, cast an oblique eye, and then discharge volleys of silvery laughter.

III

The person who best typified the comic spirit was the ghetto *schnorrer*, immortalized in *The King of Schnorrers*. This short work is a vivid and humorous portrayal of a fictitious character—one Manasseh Bueno Barzillai Azevedo da Costa—who lords it in the London ghetto at the close of the eighteenth century. He is a Sephardic mendicant, one who has developed begging to a fine art and who combines with his audacious effrontery unfailing resourcefulness and ready repartee.

Zangwill tells the story of the *schnorrer* in a series of episodes

---

[4] Max Eastman, *The Sense of Humor* (New York, 1922), p. 21.

that, taken together, make up a minor classic of absurdity. The *schnorrer* Manasseh is pitted against three people: first, the philanthropist Grobstock; secondly, Yankelé, a fellow *schnorrer*, a north-European Ashkenaz; and, finally, the Sephardic authorities, chiefly the Mahamad, a governing council of five elders of the synagogue. In each case, the inferior force seems actually to triumph over something higher and greater than itself.

Manasseh is an odd combination of aristocrat, intellectual and religionist. In his pride he never lets anyone forget that he is a Sephardi, that he traces his ancestry to the Spanish-Portuguese Jewish families who resettled in England in 1656 after having been expelled by Edward I in 1290. His very name, in fact, describes the properties that he possesses in abundance: scholarship, goodness, ancient family, wealth and royal connections suited to Manasseh's concept of himself. It is no wonder, therefore, that, on meeting with Joseph Grobstock, financier, East India Company director, treasurer of the Great Synagogue, and, as his German name would indicate, a solid, crude piece of common wood, Manasseh "towered above the unhappy capitalist, like an ancient prophet denouncing a swollen monarch."

This natural feeling of superiority that seems "to ooze from every pore" of Manasseh is further developed in his attitude toward the problem of work. Since he identifies *schnorring* with "aristocracy," the *schnorrer* believes that he is forbidden to betray his calling by work in any form, just as he must avoid any of the other things by which people seem to become rich and successful. Work is an uncertain, insecure way of making a living. Hence, when Yankelé ben Yitzchok, "a short *Schnorrer*, even dingier than da Costa," wishes to marry the latter's daughter, and tries to show that *schnorring* by synagogue-knocking brings in enough money to support her in style, Manasseh rebuffs him sharply. *Schnorring*, Manasseh believes, is the only occupation that is regular all year round. Only after Yankelé submits to the supreme test of *schnorring* from "a king of guzzlers and topers, and the meanest of mankind," the miser Rabbi Remorse Red-herring, does Manasseh promise to become his father-in-law.

The intended union of Manasseh's daughter with a Polish Jew excites the liveliest horror in the collective breasts of the Mahamad. The Tedesco did not pronounce Hebrew as they did, hence he was inferior. Manasseh is therefore summoned before these gentlemen who "administered the affairs of the Spanish-Portuguese community, and [whose] oligarchy would undoubtedly be a byword for all that is arbitrary and inquisitorial but for the widespread ignorance of its existence," to show cause why he has consented to give his daughter's hand to an "inferior" Ashkenazic Jew. Using his sharp intellect, with its immense freight of apt quotation, allusion to ancient documents and accumulated knowledge of the religious principles of the Jewish people, Manasseh demolishes the arguments of the Elders. He proves, first, that no ancient *Ascama* (ordinance) ever forbade a Sephardi from marrying a Tedesco; and, secondly, that the takers and not the givers of charity are the "pillars of the Synagogue." "Charity is the salt of riches," quotes Manasseh from the Talmud, "and, indeed, it is the salt that preserves your community." The Mahamad is foiled by the "quiet dignity of the beggar," who, proving the insecurity of their earthly power, routs them at the intellectual level.

With a final display of daring and bravado befitting only a king, Manasseh continues to lord it over the Elders by promising to contribute to the synagogue the unbelievable sum of six hundred pounds, which he later extorts from a whole series of victims. This final episode in his career not only earns him his royal title but a permanent income as well. Illustrating his many-sided genius a few days after the royal wedding of Deborah and Yankelé, Manasseh "struck the Chancellor breathless" by handing him a bag containing all the money he promised and "stipulating only that it should be used to purchase a life-annuity (styled the Da Costa Fund) for a poor and deserving member of the congregation." Thus Manasseh is thenceforward recognized as the King of *Schnorrers*.

IV

Surely Zangwill meant to do more in this book than relate some simple episodes in the life of a beggar. "The whole," as one critic has perceptively noted, "seems an ironic comment upon the absurdity of all human arrangements."[5] Beggary, the subject of

[5] *The King of Schnorrers*, ed. with Introductory Essay, "Jewish Humor," by Bernard I. Schilling (Hamden, Conn., 1953), p. xxxiii.

this tale, implies a long history of poverty, injustice and degradation, to which the Jew in the Diaspora has been subjected. To offset the grim realities of the ghetto, there arose from the soil of Jewish life a bent to self-criticism that Freud called "tendency-wit." Humorous tales, subtle comments, witty anecdotes were directed, at times, against oneself, at other times, "against a person in whom one takes interest, that is, a composite personality such as one's own people."[6] These stories, invented by Jews themselves, mocked Jewish peculiarities and shortcomings and thus provided much psychic relief for the downtrodden of the ghetto. "From death and beggary themselves the Jews extracted the ludicrous."[7] Social stability, then, was achieved in the ghetto through "wise laughter."

And wisdom is the key to the understanding of Manasseh's life and mind. Faced with the absurdities of the ghetto in which a learned man is considered inferior, Manasseh exaggerates his own value in order to build up his position among men who, for the moment, appear vastly superior. In this effort to achieve prominence he uses his intellect, which, because of his close study and vast knowledge of the Talmud, has been sharpened to deal ingeniously with all the vexing problems confronting him. Being more learned, Manasseh refuses to recognize any difference between master and servant, and insists, as Freud also recognized, "that the rich man gives him nothing, since he is obligated by [religious] mandate to give alms, and strictly speaking must be thankful that the schnorrer gives him an opportunity to be charitable."[8] Such arguments, at once audacious and humorous, offered psychic relief for all those anxious mendicants who, like Manasseh, roamed the streets of the ghetto in search of help.

The King of Schnorrers, therefore, underscores that special quality of Jewish humor that cures folly with folly and like the comic spirit, makes game of "serious" life. Manasseh's humor is "something intellectually quick whereby acuteness of mind may triumph over the actual facts and grim problems of life. Things

6 Sigmund Freud, *Jokes and Their Relation to the Unconscious. Complete Psychological Works,* ed. James Strachey (London, 1960), VIII, 111. My translation of the original varies slightly from that of Mr. Strachey.

7 Schilling, *op. cit.,* p. viii.

8 Freud, *op. cit.,* p. 113.

are endurable only if the mind can find a twist, an element of relief or humor, to obscure the hopeless wretchedness of life as it often is. So once more the Jews have been able better to accept life in the face of what it has done to them."[9] Heart *and* mind laugh with the King of *Schnorrers.*

Comedy heightened Zangwill's consciousness of the tragic element in ghetto life. If, for example, Manasseh acts absurdly, if he has to use his mental skill to overpower his adversaries, it is only because these adversaries need to be overpowered. If, in short, his antics make us laugh, they also make us cry. Why? Because within the narrow radius of the ghetto reside a group of people who, as a result of the vicissitudes of migration and in spite of their tradition, worship the gruff, pompous, parsimonious financiers instead of the learned, the scholars, the intellectuals. Secondly, these very people who bear the cross of discrimination gain the dubious distinction of discriminating against their own brethren by forbidding, for example, a Sephardi to marry a Tedesco. And, finally, what seems far worse, we find Manasseh, who refuses himself to distinguish between master and servant, looking with disfavor on Yankelé, a fellow mendicant, until the latter proves his worth as a *schnorrer.* It is this theme—disunity among Jews in the face of adversity, and their loss of a sense of values—that preoccupied so much of Zangwill's mind and art, particularly in *The King of Schnorrers.*

MAURICE WOHLGELERNTER

December 20, 1964
New York City

---

[9] Schilling, *op. cit.,* p. xxix.

This new Dover edition
is dedicated
to
TOBIAS HELLER
and
the memory of
ARTHUR H. HELLER

FROM THE AUTHOR'S FOREWORD

These episodes make no claim to veracity, while the personages are not even sun-myths. I have merely amused myself and attempted to amuse idlers by incarnating the floating tradition of the Jewish *Schnorrer*, who is as unique among beggars as Israel among nations. The close of the eighteenth century was chosen for a background, because, while the most picturesque period of Anglo-Jewish history, it has never before been exploited in fiction, whether by novelists or historians.

CONTENTS

That all men are beggars, 'tis very plain to see,
Though some they are of lowly, and some of high degree:
Your ministers of State will say they never will allow
That kings from subjects beg; but that you know is all bow-wow.
Bow-wow-wow! Fol lol, etc.

OLD PLAY.

CHAPTER I

SHOWING HOW THE WICKED PHILANTHROPIST WAS
TURNED INTO A FISH-PORTER

In the days when Lord George Gordon became a Jew, and was
suspected of insanity; when, out of respect for the prophecies,
England denied her Jews every civic right except that of paying
taxes; when the *Gentleman's Magazine* had ill words for the
infidel alien; when Jewish marriages were invalid and bequests
for Hebrew colleges void; when a prophet prophesying Primrose
Day would have been set in the stocks, though Pitt inclined his
private ear to Benjamin Goldsmid's views on the foreign loans —
in those days, when Tevele Schiff was Rabbi in Israel, and Dr.
de Falk, the Master of the Tetragrammaton, saint and Cab-
balistic conjuror, flourished in Wellclose Square, and the com-
poser of "The Death of Nelson" was a choir-boy in the Great
Synagogue; Joseph Grobstock, pillar of the same, emerged one
afternoon into the spring sunshine at the fag-end of the de-
parting stream of worshippers. In his hand was a large canvas
bag, and in his eye a twinkle.

There had been a special service of prayer and thanksgiving
for the happy restoration of his Majesty's health, and the cantor
had interceded tunefully with Providence on behalf of Royal
George and "our most amiable Queen, Charlotte." The congregation was large and fashionable — far more so than when only
a heavenly sovereign was concerned — and so the courtyard was
thronged with a string of *Schnorrers* (beggars), awaiting the exit
of the audience, much as the vestibule of the opera-house is lined
by footmen.

They were a motley crew, with tangled beards and long hair that fell in curls, if not the curls of the period; but the gaberdines of the German Ghettoes had been in most cases exchanged for the knee-breeches and many-buttoned jacket of the Londoner. When the clothes one has brought from the Continent wear out, one must needs adopt the attire of one's superiors, or be reduced to buying. Many bore staves, and had their loins girded up with coloured handkerchiefs, as though ready at any moment to return from the Captivity. Their woebegone air was achieved almost entirely by not washing — it owed little to nature, to adventitious aids in the shape of deformities. The merest sprinkling boasted of physical afflictions, and none exposed sores like the lazars of Italy or contortions like the cripples of Constantinople. Such crude methods are eschewed in the fine art of *schnorring*. A green shade might denote weakness of sight, but the stone-blind man bore no braggart placard — his infirmity was an old established concern well known to the public, and conferring upon the proprietor a definite status in the community. He was no anonymous atom, such as drifts blindly through Christendom, vagrant and apologetic. Rarest of all sights in this pageantry of Jewish pauperdom was the hollow trouser-leg or the empty sleeve, or the wooden limb fulfilling either and pushing out a proclamatory peg.

When the pack of *Schnorrers* caught sight of Joseph Grobstock, they fell upon him full-cry, blessing him. He, nothing surprised, brushed pompously through the benedictions, though the twinkle in his eye became a roguish gleam. Outside the iron gates, where the throng was thickest, and where some elegant chariots that had brought worshippers from distant Hackney were preparing to start, he came to a standstill, surrounded by clamouring *Schnorrers,* and dipped his hand slowly and ceremoniously into the bag. There was a moment of breathless expectation among the beggars, and Joseph Grobstock had a moment of exquisite consciousness of importance, as he stood there swelling in the sunshine. There was no middle class to speak of in the eighteenth-century Jewry; the world was divided into rich and poor, and the rich were very, very rich, and the poor very, very poor, so that everyone knew his station. Joseph Grobstock was satisfied with that in which it had pleased God to place him. He was a jovial, heavy-jowled creature, whose clean-shaven chin was doubling, and he was habited like a person of the first respectability in a beautiful blue body-coat with a row of big yellow buttons. The frilled shirt front, high collar of the very newest fashion, and copious white neckerchief showed off the massive fleshiness of the red throat. His hat was of the Quaker pattern, and his head did not fail of the periwig and the pigtail, the latter being heretical in name only.

What Joseph Grobstock drew from the bag was a small white-paper packet, and his sense of humour led him to place it in the hand furthest from his nose; for it was a broad humour, not a subtle. It enabled him to extract pleasure from seeing a fellow-mortal's hat rollick in the wind, but did little to alleviate the chase for his own. His jokes clapped you on the back, they did not tickle delicately.

Such was the man who now became the complacent cynosure of all eyes, even of those that had no appeal in them, as soon as the principle of his eleemosynary operations had broken on the crowd. The first *Schnorrer*, feverishly tearing open his package, had found a florin, and, as by electricity, all except the blind beggar were aware that Joseph Grobstock was distributing florins. The distributor partook of the general consciousness, and his lips twitched. Silently he dipped again into the bag, and, selecting the hand nearest, put a second white package into it. A wave of joy brightened the grimy face, to change instantly to one of horror.

"You have made a mistake — you have given me a penny!" cried the beggar.

"Keep it for your honesty," replied Joseph Grobstock imperturbably, and affected not to enjoy the laughter of the rest. The third mendicant ceased laughing when he discovered that fold on fold of paper sheltered a tiny sixpence. It was now obvious that the great man was distributing prize-packets, and the excitement of the piebald crowd grew momently. Grobstock went on dipping, lynx-eyed against second applications. One of the few pieces of gold in the lucky-bag fell to the solitary lame man, who danced in his joy on his sound leg, while the poor blind man pocketed his half-penny, unconscious of ill-fortune, and merely wondering why the coin came swathed in paper.

By this time Grobstock could control his face no longer, and the last episodes of the lottery were played to the accompaniment of a broad grin. Keen and complex was his enjoyment. There was not only the general surprise at this novel feat of alms; there were the special surprises of detail written on face after face, as it flashed or fell or frowned in congruity with the contents of the envelope, and for undercurrent a delicious hubbub of interjections and benedictions, a stretching and withdrawing of palms, and a swift shifting of figures, that made the scene a farrago of excitements. So that the broad grin was one of gratification as well as of amusement, and part of the gratification sprang from a real kindliness of heart — for Grobstock was an easy-going man with whom the world had gone easy. The *Schnorrers* were exhausted before the packets, but the philanthropist was in no anxiety to be rid of the remnant. Closing the mouth of the considerably lightened bag and clutching it tightly by the throat, and recomposing his face to gravity, he moved slowly down the street like a stately treasure-ship flecked by the sunlight. His way led towards Goodman's Fields, where his mansion was situate, and he knew that the fine weather would bring out *Schnorrers* enough. And, indeed, he had not gone many paces before he met a figure he did not remember having seen before.

Leaning against a post at the head of the narrow passage which led to Bevis Marks was a tall, black-bearded, turbaned personage, a first glance at whom showed him of the true tribe. Mechanically Joseph Grobstock's hand went to the lucky-bag, and he drew out a neatly-folded packet and tendered it to the stranger.

The stranger received the gift graciously, and opened it gravely, the philanthropist loitering awkwardly to mark the issue. Suddenly the dark face became a thunder-cloud, the eyes flashed lightning.

"An evil spirit in your ancestors' bones!" hissed the stranger, from between his flashing teeth. "Did you come here to insult me?"

"Pardon, a thousand pardons!" stammered the magnate, wholly taken aback. "I fancied you were a — a — a — poor man."

"And, therefore, you came to insult me!"

"No, no, I thought to help you," murmured Grobstock, turning from red to scarlet. Was it possible he had foisted his charity upon an undeserving millionaire? No! Through all the clouds of his own confusion and the recipient's anger, the figure of a *Schnorrer* loomed too plain for mistake. None but a *Schnorrer* would wear a home-made turban, issue of a black cap crossed with a white kerchief; none but a *Schnorrer* would unbutton the first nine buttons of his waistcoat, or, if this relaxation were due to the warmth of the weather, counteract it by wearing an over-garment, especially one as heavy as a blanket, with buttons the size of compasses and flaps reaching nearly to his shoe-buckles, even though its length were only congruous with that of his undercoat, which already reached the bottoms of his knee-breeches. Finally, who but a *Schnorrer* would wear this overcoat cloak-wise, with dangling sleeves, full of armless suggestion from a side view? Quite apart from the shabbiness of the snuff-coloured fabric, it was amply evident that the wearer did not dress by rule or measure. Yet the disproportions of his attire did but enhance the picturesqueness of a personality that would be striking even in a bath, though it was not likely to be seen there. The beard was jet black, sweeping and unkempt, and ran up his cheeks to meet the raven hair, so that the vivid face was framed in black; it was a long, tapering face with sanguine lips gleaming at the heart of a black bush; the eyes were large and lambent, set in deep sockets under black arching eyebrows; the nose was long and Coptic; the brow low but broad, with straggling wisps of hair protruding from beneath the turban. His right hand grasped a plain ashen staff.

Worthy Joseph Grobstock found the figure of the mendicant only too impressive; he shrank uneasily before the indignant eyes.

"I meant to help you," he repeated.

"And this is how one helps a brother in Israel?" said the *Schnorrer*, throwing the paper contemptuously into the philanthropist's face. It struck him on the bridge of the nose, but impinged so mildly that he felt at once what was the matter. The packet was empty — the *Schnorrer* had drawn a blank; the only one the good-natured man had put into the bag.

The *Schnorrer's* audacity sobered Joseph Grobstock completely; it might have angered him to chastise the fellow, but it did not. His better nature prevailed; he began to feel shame-faced, fumbled sheepishly in his pocket for a crown; then hesitated, as fearing this peace-offering would not altogether suffice with so rare a spirit, and that he owed the stranger more than silver — an apology to wit. He proceeded honestly to pay it, but with a maladroit manner, as one unaccustomed to the currency.

"You are an impertinent rascal," he said, "but I daresay you feel hurt. Let me assure you I did not know there was nothing in the packet. I did not, indeed."

"Then your steward has robbed me!" exclaimed the *Schnorrer* excitedly. "You let him make up the packets, and he has stolen my money — the thief, the transgressor, thrice-cursed who robs the poor."

"You don't understand," interrupted the magnate meekly. "I made up the packets myself."

"Then, why do you say you did not know what was in them? Go, you mock my misery!"

"Nay, hear me out!" urged Grobstock desperately. "In some I placed gold, in the greater number silver, in a few copper, in one alone — nothing. That is the one you have drawn. It is your misfortune."

"*My* misfortune!" echoed the *Schnorrer* scornfully. "It is *your* misfortune — I did not even draw it. The Holy One, blessed be He, has punished you for your heartless jesting with the poor — making a sport for yourself of their misfortunes, even as the Philistines sported with Samson. The good deed you might have put to your account by a gratuity to me, God has taken from you. He has declared you unworthy of achieving righteousness through me. Go your way, murderer!"

"Murderer!" repeated the philanthropist, bewildered by this harsh view of his action.

"Yes, murderer! Stands it not in the Talmud that he who shames another is as one who spills his blood? And have you not put me to shame — if anyone had witnessed your almsgiving, would he not have laughed in my beard?"

The pillar of the Synagogue felt as if his paunch were shrinking.

"But the others — " he murmured deprecatingly. "I have not shed their blood — have I not given freely of my hard-earned gold?"

"For your own diversion," retorted the *Schnorrer* implacably. "But what says the Midrash? There is a wheel rolling in the world — not he who is rich to-day is rich to-morrow, but this one

He brings up, and this one He brings down, as is said in the seventy-fifth Psalm. Therefore, lift not up your horn on high, nor speak with a stiff neck."

He towered above the unhappy capitalist, like an ancient prophet denouncing a swollen monarch. The poor man put his hand involuntarily to his high collar as if to explain away his apparent arrogance, but in reality because he was not breathing easily under the *Schnorrer's* attack.

"You are an uncharitable man," he panted hotly, driven to a line of defence he had not anticipated. "I did it not from wantonness, but from faith in Heaven. I know well that God sits turning a wheel — therefore I did not presume to turn it myself. Did I not let Providence select who should have the silver and who the gold, who the copper and who the emptiness? Besides, God alone knows who really needs my assistance — I have made Him my almoner; I have cast my burden on the Lord."

"Epicurean!" shrieked the *Schnorrer*. "Blasphemer! Is it thus you would palter with the sacred texts? Do you forget what the next verse says: 'Bloodthirsty and deceitful men shall not live out half their days'? Shame on you — you a *Gabbai* (treasurer) of the Great Synagogue. You see I know you, Joseph Grobstock. Has not the beadle of your Synagogue boasted to me that you have given him a guinea for brushing your spatterdashes? Would you think of offering *him* a packet? Nay, it is the poor that are trodden on — they whose merits are in excess of those of beadles. But the Lord will find others to take up his loans — for he who hath pity on the poor lendeth to the Lord. You are no true son of Israel."

The *Schnorrer's* tirade was long enough to allow Grobstock to recover his dignity and his breath.

"If you really knew me, you would know that the Lord is considerably in my debt," he rejoined quietly. "When next you would discuss me, speak with the Psalms-men, not the beadle. Never have I neglected the needy. Even now, though you have been insolent and uncharitable, I am ready to befriend you if you are in want."

"If I am in want!" repeated the Schorrer scornfully. "Is there anything I do not want?"

"You are married?"

"You correct me — wife and children are the only things I do *not* lack."

"No pauper does," quoth Grobstock, with a twinkle of restored humour.

"No," assented the *Schnorrer* sternly. "The poor man has the fear of Heaven. He obeys the Law and the Commandments. He marries while he is young — and his spouse is not cursed with barrenness. It is the rich man who transgresses the Judgment, who delays to come under the Canopy."

"Ah! well, here is a guinea — in the name of my wife," broke in Grobstock laughingly. "Or stay — since you do not brush spatterdashes — here is another."

"In the name of my wife," rejoined the *Schnorrer* with dignity, "I thank you."

"Thank me in your own name," said Grobstock. "I mean tell it me."

"I am Manasseh Bueno Barzillai Azevedo da Costa," he answered simply.

"A Sephardi!" exclaimed the philanthropist.

"Is it not written on my face, even as it is written on yours that you are a Tedesco? It is the first time that I have taken gold from one of your lineage."

"Oh, indeed!" murmured Grobstock, beginning to feel small again.

"Yes — are we not far richer than your community? What need have I to take the good deeds away from my own people — they have too few opportunities for beneficence as it is, being so many of them wealthy; brokers and West India merchants, and — "

"But I, too, am a financier, and an East India Director," Grobstock reminded him.

"Maybe; but your community is yet young and struggling — your rich men are as the good men in Sodom for multitude. You are the immigrants of yesterday — refugees from the Ghettoes of Russia and Poland and Germany. But we, as you are aware, have been established here for generations; in the Peninsula our ancestors graced the courts of kings, and controlled the purse-strings of princes; in Holland we held the empery of trade. Ours have been the poets and scholars in Israel. You cannot expect that we should recognise your rabble, which prejudices us in the eyes of England. We made the name of Jew honourable; you degrade it. You are as the mixed multitude which came up with our forefathers out of Egypt."

"Nonsense!" said Grobstock sharply. "All Israel are brethren."

"Esau was the brother of Israel," answered Manasseh sententiously. "But you will excuse me if I go a-marketing, it is such a pleasure to handle gold." There was a note of wistful pathos in the latter remark which took off the edge of the former, and touched Joseph with compunction for bandying words with a hungry man whose loved ones were probably starving patiently at home.

"Certainly, haste away," he said kindly.

"I shall see you again," said Manasseh, with a valedictory wave of his hand, and digging his staff into the cobblestones he journeyed forwards without bestowing a single backward glance upon his benefactor.

Grobstock's road took him to Petticoat Lane in the wake of Manasseh. He had no intention of following him, but did not see why he should change his route for fear of the *Schnorrer,* more especially as Manasseh did not look back. By this time he had become conscious again of the bag he carried, but he had no heart to proceed with the fun. He felt conscience stricken, and had recourse to his pockets instead in his progress through the narrow jostling market-street, where he scarcely ever bought anything personally save fish and good deeds. He was a connoisseur in both. To-day he picked up many a good deed cheap, paying pennies for articles he did not take away — shoe-latchets and cane-strings, barley-sugar and butter-cakes. Suddenly, through a chink in an opaque mass of human beings, he caught sight of a small attractive salmon on a fishmonger's slab. His eye glittered, his chops watered. He elbowed his way to the vendor, whose eye caught a corresponding gleam, and whose finger went to his hat in respectful greeting.

"Good afternoon, Jonathan," said Grobstock jovially, "I'll take that salmon there — how much?"

"Pardon me," said a voice in the crowd, "I am just bargaining for it."

Grobstock started. It was the voice of Manasseh.

"Stop that nonsense, da Costa," responded the fishmonger. "You know you won't give me my price. It is the only one I have left," he added, half for the benefit of Grobstock. "I couldn't let it go under a couple of guineas."

"Here's your money," cried Manasseh with passionate contempt, and sent two golden coins spinning musically upon the slab.

In the crowd sensation, in Grobstock's breast astonishment, indignation, and bitterness. He was struck momentarily dumb. His face purpled. The scales of the salmon shone like a celestial vision that was fading from him by his own stupidity.

"I'll take that salmon, Jonathan," he repeated, spluttering. "Three guineas."

"Pardon me," repeated Manasseh, "it is too late. This is not an auction." He seized the fish by the tail.

Grobstock turned upon him, goaded to the point of apoplexy. "You!" he cried. "You — you — rogue! How dare you buy salmon!"

"Rogue yourself!" retorted Manasseh. "Would you have me steal salmon?"

"You have stolen my money, knave, rascal!"

"Murderer! Shedder of blood! Did you not give me the money as a free-will offering, for the good of your wife's soul? I call on you before all these witnesses to confess yourself a slanderer!"

"Slanderer, indeed! I repeat, you are a knave and a jackanapes. You — a pauper — a beggar — with a wife and children. How can you have the face to go and spend two guineas — two whole guineas — all you have in the world — on a mere luxury like salmon?"

Manasseh elevated his arched eyebrows.

"If I do not buy salmon when I have two guineas," he answered quietly, "when shall I buy salmon? As you say, it is a luxury; very dear. It is only on rare occasions like this that my means run to it." There was a dignified pathos about the rebuke that mollified the magnate. He felt that there was reason in the beggar's point of view — though it was a point to which he would never himself have risen, unaided. But righteous anger still simmered in him; he felt vaguely that there was something to be said in reply, though he also felt that even if he knew what it was, it would have to be said in a lower key to correspond with Manasseh's transition from the high pitch of the opening passages. Not finding the requisite repartee he was silent.

"In the name of my wife," went on Manasseh, swinging the salmon by the tail, "I ask you to clear my good name which you have bespattered in the presence of my very tradesmen. Again I call upon you to confess before these witnesses that you gave me the money yourself in charity. Come! Do you deny it?"

"No, I don't deny it," murmured Grobstock, unable to understand why he appeared to himself like a whipped cur, or how what should have been a boast had been transformed into an apology to a beggar.

"In the name of my wife, I thank you," said Manasseh. "She loves salmon, and fries with unction. And now, since you have no further use for that bag of yours, I will relieve you of its burden by taking my salmon home in it." He took the canvas bag from the limp grasp of the astonished Tedesco, and dropped the fish in. The head protruded, surveying the scene with a cold, glassy, ironical eye.

"Good afternoon all," said the *Schnorrer* courteously.

"One moment," called out the philanthropist, when he found his tongue. "The bag is not empty — there are a number of packets still left in it."

"So much the better!" said Manasseh soothingly. "You will be saved from the temptation to continue shedding the blood of the poor, and I shall be saved from spending *all* your bounty upon salmon — an extravagance you were right to deplore."

"But—but!" began Grobstock.

"No — no 'buts,' " protested Manasseh, waving his bag deprecatingly. "You were right. You admitted you were wrong before; shall I be less magnaminous now? In the presence of all these witnesses I acknowledge the justice of your rebuke. I ought not to have wasted two guineas on one fish. It was not worth it. Come over here, and I will tell you something." He walked out of earshot of the bystanders, turning down a side alley opposite the stall, and beckoned with his salmon bag. The East India Director had no course but to obey. He would probably have followed him in any case, to have it out with him, but now he had a humiliating sense of being at the *Schnorrer's* beck and call.

"Well, what more have you to say?" he demanded gruffly.

"I wish to save you money in future," said the beggar in low, confidential tones. "That Jonathan is a son of the separation! The salmon is not worth two guineas — no, on my soul! If you had not come up I should have got it for twenty-five shillings. Jonathan stuck on the price when he thought you would buy. I trust you will not let me be the loser by your arrival, and that if I should find less than seventeen shillings in the bag you will make it up to me."

The bewildered financier felt his grievance disappearing as by sleight of hand.

Manasseh added winningly: "I know you are a gentleman, capable of behaving as finely as any Sephardi."

This handsome compliment completed the *Schnorrer's* victory, which was sealed by his saying, "And so I should not like you to have it on your soul that you had done a poor man out of a few shillings."

Grobstock could only remark meekly: "You will find more than seventeen shillings in the bag."

"Ah, why were you born a Tedesco!" cried Manasseh ecstatically. "Do you know what I have a mind to do? To come and be your Sabbath-guest! Yes, I will take supper with you next Friday, and we will welcome the Bride — the holy Sabbath — together! Never before have I sat at the table of a Tedesco — but you — you are a man after my own heart. Your soul is a son of Spain. Next Friday at six — do not forget."

"But — but I do not have Sabbath-guests," faltered Grobstock.

"Not have Sabbath-guests! No, no, I will not believe you are of the sons of Belial, whose table is spread only for the rich, who do not proclaim your equality with the poor even once a week. It is your fine nature that would hide its benefactions. Do not I, Manasseh Bueno Barzillai Azevedo da Costa, have at my Sabbath-table every week Yankelé ben Yitzchok — a Pole? And if I have a Tedesco at my table, why should I draw the line there? Why should I not permit you, a Tedesco, to return the hospitality to me, a Sephardi? At six, then! I know your house well — it is an elegant building that does credit to your taste — do not be uneasy — I shall not fail to be punctual. *A Dios!*"

This time he waved his stick fraternally, and stalked down a turning. For an instant Grobstock stood glued to the spot, crushed by a sense of the inevitable. Then a horrible thought occurred to him.

Easy-going man as he was, he might put up with the visitation of Manasseh. But then he had a wife, and, what was worse, a livery servant. How could he expect a livery servant to tolerate such a guest? He might fly from the town on Friday evening, but that would necessitate troublesome explanations. And Manasseh would come again the next Friday. That was certain. Manasseh would be like grim death — his coming, though it might be postponed, was inevitable. Oh, it was too terrible. At all costs he must revoke the invitation (?). Placed between Scylla and Charybdis, between Manasseh and his manservant, he felt he could sooner face the former.

"Da Costa!" he called in agony. "Da Costa!"

The *Schnorrer* turned, and then Grobstock found he was mistaken in imagining he preferred to face da Costa.

"You called me?" enquired the beggar.

"Y — e — s," faltered the East India Director, and stood paralysed.

"What can I do for you?" said Manasseh graciously.

"Would you mind — very much — if I — if I asked you — "

"Not to come," was in his throat, but stuck there.

"If you asked me — " said Manasseh encouragingly.

"To accept some of my clothes," flashed Grobstock, with a sudden inspiration. After all, Manasseh was a fine figure of a man. If he could get him to doff those musty garments of his he might almost pass him off as a prince of the blood, foreign by his beard — at any rate he could be certain of making him acceptable to the livery servant. He breathed freely again at this happy solution of the situation.

"Your cast-off clothes?" asked Manasseh. Grobstock was not sure whether the tone was supercilious or eager. He hastened to explain. "No, not quite that. Secondhand things I am still wearing. My old clothes were already given away at Passover to Simeon the Psalms-man. These are comparatively new."

"Then I would beg you to excuse me," said Manasseh, with a stately wave of the bag.

"Oh, but why not?" murmured Grobstock, his blood running cold again.

"I cannot," said Manasseh, shaking his head.

"But they will just about fit you," pleaded the philanthropist.

"That makes it all the more absurd for you to give them to

Simeon the Psalms-man," said Manasseh sternly. "Still, since he is your clothes-receiver, I could not think of interfering with his office. It is not etiquette. I am surprised you should ask me if I should mind. Of course I should mind — I should mind very much."

"But he is not my clothes-receiver," protested Grobstock. "Last Passover was the first time I gave them to him, because my cousin Hyman Rosenstein, who used to have them, has died."

"But surely he considers himself your cousin's heir," said Manasseh. "He expects all your clothes henceforth."

"No. I gave him no such promise."

Manasseh hesitated.

"Well, in that case —"

"In that case," repeated Grobstock breathlessly.

"On condition that I am to have the appointment permanently, of course."

. "Of course," echoed Grobstock eagerly.

"Because you see," Manasseh condescended to explain, "it hurts one's reputation to lose a client."

"Yes, yes, naturally," said Grobstock soothingly. "I quite understand." Then, feeling himself slipping into future embarrassments, he added timidly, "Of course they will not always be so good as the first lot, because — "

"Say no more," Manasseh interrupted reassuringly, "I will come at once and fetch them."

"No. I will send them," cried Grobstock, horrified afresh.

"I could not dream of permitting it. What! Shall I put you to all that trouble which should rightly be mine? I will go at once — the matter shall be settled without delay, I promise you; as it is written, 'I made haste and delayed not!' Follow me!" Grobstock suppressed a groan. Here had all his manœuvering landed him in a worse plight than ever. He would have to present Manasseh to the livery servant without even that clean face which might not unreasonably have been expected for the Sabbath. Despite the text quoted by the erudite *Schnorrer,* he strove to put off the evil hour.

"Had you not better take the salmon home to your wife first?" said he.

"My duty is to enable you to complete your good deed at once. My wife is unaware of the salmon. She is in no suspense."

Even as the *Schnorrer* spake it flashed upon Grobstock that Manasseh was more presentable with the salmon than without it — in fact, that the salmon was the salvation of the situation. When Grobstock bought fish he often hired a man to carry home the spoil. Manasseh would have all the air of such a loafer. Who would suspect that the fish and even the bag belonged to the porter, though purchased with the gentleman's money? Grobstock silently thanked Providence for the ingenious way in which it had contrived to save his self-respect. As a mere fish-carrier Manasseh would attract no second glance from the household; once safely in, it would be comparatively easy to smuggle him out, and when he did come on Friday night it would be in the metamorphosing glories of a body-coat, with his unspeakable undergarment turned into a shirt and his turban knocked into a cocked hat.

They emerged into Aldgate, and then turned down Leman Street, a fashionable quarter, and so into Great Prescott Street. At the critical street corner Grobstock's composure began to desert him; he took out his handsomely ornamented snuff-box and administered to himself a mighty pinch. It did him good, and he walked on and was well nigh arrived at his own door when Manasseh suddenly caught him by a coat button.

"Stand still a second," he cried imperatively.

"What is it?" murmured Grobstock, in alarm.

"You have spilt snuff all down your coat front," Manasseh replied severely. "Hold the bag a moment while I brush it off."

Joseph obeyed, and Manasseh scrupulously removed every particle with such patience that Grobstock's was exhausted.

"Thank you," he said at last, as politely as he could. "That will do."

"No, it will not do," replied Manasseh. "I cannot have my coat spoiled. By the time it comes to me it will be a mass of stains if I don't look after it."

"Oh, is that why you took so much trouble?" said Grobstock, with an uneasy laugh.

"Why else? Do you take me for a beadle, a brusher of gaiters?" enquired Manasseh haughtily. "There now! that is the cleanest I can get it. You would escape those droppings if you held your snuff-box so — " Manasseh gently took the snuff-box and began to explain, walking on a few paces.

"Ah, we are at home!" he cried, breaking off the object-lesson suddenly. He pushed open the gate, ran up the steps of the mansion and knocked thunderously, then snuffed himself magnificently from the bejewelled snuff-box.

Behind came Joseph Grobstock, slouching limply, and carrying Manasseh da Costa's fish.

CHAPTER II

SHOWING HOW THE KING REIGNED

When he realised that he had been turned into a fish-porter, the financier hastened up the steps so as to be at the *Schnorrer's* side when the door opened.

The livery servant was visibly taken aback by the spectacle of their juxtaposition.

"This salmon to the cook!" cried Gdobstock desperately, handing him the bag.

Da Costa looked thunders, and was about to speak, but Grobstock's eye sought his in frantic appeal. "Wait a minute; I will settle with you," he cried, congratulating himself on a phrase that would carry another meaning to Wilkinson's ears. He drew a breath of relief when the flunkey disappeared, and left them standing in the spacious hall with its statues and plants.

"Is this the way you steal my salmon, after all?" demanded da Costa hotly.

"Hush, hush! I didn't mean to steal it! I will pay you for it!"

"I refuse to sell! You coveted it from the first — you have broken the Tenth Commandment, even as these stone figures violate the Second. Your invitation to me to accompany you here at once was a mere trick. Now I understand why you were so eager."

"No, no, da Costa. Seeing that you placed the fish in my hands, I had no option but to give it to Wilkinson, because — because — " Grobstock would have had some difficulty in explaining, but Manasseh saved him the pain.

"You had to give *my* fish to Wilkinson!" he interrupted. "Sir,

I thought you were a fine man, a man of honour. I admit that I placed my fish in your hands. But because I had no hesitation in allowing you to carry it, this is how you repay my confidence!"

In the whirl of his thoughts Grobstock grasped at the word "repay" as a swimmer in a whirlpool grasps at a straw.

"I will repay your money!" he cried. "Here are your two guineas. You will get another salmon, and more cheaply. As you pointed out, you could have got this for twenty-five shillings."

"Two guineas!" ejaculated Manasseh contemptuously. "Why you offered Jonathan, the fishmonger, three!"

Grobstock was astounded, but it was beneath him to bargain. And he remembered that, after all, he *would* enjoy the salmon.

"Well, here are three guineas," he said pacifically, offering them.

"Three guineas!" echoed Manasseh, spurning them. "And what of my profit?"

"Profit!" gasped Grobstock.

"Since you have made me a middle-man, since you have forced me into the fish trade, I must have my profits like anybody else."

"Here is a crown extra!"

"And my compensation?"

"What do you mean?" enquired Grobstock, exasperated. "Compensation for what?"

"For what? For two things at the very least," Manasseh said unswervingly. "In the first place," and as he began his logically divided reply his tone assumed the sing-song sacred to Talmudical dialectics, "compensation for not eating the salmon myself. For it is not as if I offered it you — I merely entrusted it to you, and it is ordained in Exodus that if a man shall deliver unto his neighbour an ass, or an ox, or a sheep, or any beast to keep, then for every matter of trespass, whether it be for ox, for ass, for sheep, for raiment, or for any manner of lost thing, the man shall receive double, and therefore you should pay me six guineas. And secondly —"

"Not another farthing!" spluttered Grobstock, red as a turkey-cock.

"Very well," said the *Schnorrer* imperturbably, and, lifting up his voice, he called "Wilkinson!"

"Hush!" commanded Grobstock. "What are you doing?"

"I will tell Wilkinson to bring back my property."

"Wilkinson will not obey you."

"Not obey *me!* A servant! Why he is not even black! All the Sephardim I visit have black pages — much grander than Wilkinson — and they tremble at my nod. At Baron D'Aguilar's mansion in Broad Street Buildings there is a retinue of twenty-four servants, and they —"

"And what is your second claim?"

"Compensation for being degraded to fishmongering. I am not of those who sell things in the streets. I am a son of the Law, a student of the Talmud."

"If a crown piece will satisfy each of these claims —"

"I am not a blood-sucker — as it is said in the Talmud, Tractate Passover, 'God loves the man who gives not way to wrath nor stickles for his rights' — that makes altogether three guineas and three crowns."

"Yes. Here they are."

Wilkinson reappeared. "You called me, sir?" he said.

"No, *I* called you," said Manasseh, "I wished to give you a crown."

And he handed him one of the three. Wilkinson took it, stupefied, and retired.

"Did I not get rid of him cleverly?" said Manasseh. "You see how he obeys me!"

"Ye-es."

"I shall not ask you for more than the bare crown I gave him to save your honour."

"To save my honour!"

"Would you have had me tell him the real reason I called him was that his master was a thief? No, sir, I was careful not to shed your blood in public, though you had no such care for mine."

"Here is the crown!" said Grobstock savagely. "Nay, here are three!" He turned out his breeches-pockets to exhibit their absolute nudity.

"No, no," said Manasseh mildly, "I shall take but two. You had best keep the other — you may want a little silver." He pressed it into the magnate's hand.

"You should not be so prodigal in future," he added, in kindly approach. "It is bad to be left with nothing to one's pocket — I know the feeling, and can sympathise with you." Grobstock stood speechless, clasping the crown of charity.

Standing thus at the hall door, he had the air of Wilkinson, surprised by a too generous vail.

Da Costa cut short the crisis by offering his host a pinch from the jewel-crusted snuff-box. Grobstock greedily took the whole box, the beggar resigning it to him without protest. In his gratitude for this unexpected favour, Grobstock pocketed the silver insult without further ado, and led the way towards the second-hand clothes. He walked gingerly, so as not to awaken his wife, who was a great amateur of the siesta, and might issue suddenly from her apartment like a spider, but Manasseh stolidly thumped on the stairs with his staff. Happily the carpet was thick.

The clothes hung in a mahogany wardrobe with a plate-glass front in Grobstock's elegantly appointed bedchamber.

Grobstock rummaged among them while Manasseh, parting the white Persian curtains lined with pale pink, gazed out of the window towards the Tenterground that stretched in the rear of the mansion. Leaning on his staff, he watched the couples promenading among the sunlit parterres and amid the shrubberies, in the cool freshness of declining day. Here and there the vivid face of a dark-eyed beauty gleamed like a passion-flower. Manasseh surveyed the scene with bland benevolence; at peace with God and man.

He did not deign to bestow a glance upon the garments till Grobstock observed: "There! I think that's all I can spare." Then he turned leisurely and regarded — with the same benign aspect — the litter Grobstock had spread upon the bed — a medley of articles in excellent condition, gorgeous neckerchiefs piled in three-cornered hats, and buckled shoes trampling on white waistcoats. But his eye had scarcely rested on them a quarter of a minute when a sudden flash came into it, and a spasm crossed his face.

"Excuse me!" he cried, and hastened towards the door.

"What's the matter?" exclaimed Grobstock, in astonished apprehension. Was his gift to be flouted thus?

"I'll be back in a moment," said Manasseh, and hurried down the stairs.

Relieved on one point, Grobstock was still full of vague alarms.

He ran out on the landing. "What do you want?" he called down as loudly as he dared.

"My money!" said Manasseh.

Imagining that the *Schnorrer* had left the proceeds of the sale of the salmon in the hall, Joseph Grobstock returned to his room, and occupied himself half-mechanically in sorting the garments he had thrown higgledy-piggledy upon the bed. In so doing he espied amid the heap a pair of pantaloons entirely new and unworn which he had carelessly thrown in. It was while replacing this in the wardrobe that he heard sounds of objurgation. The cook's voice — Hibernian and high-pitched — travelled unmistakably to his ears, and brought fresh trepidation to his heart. He repaired to the landing again, and craned his neck over the balustrade. Happily the sounds were evanescent; in another minute Manasseh's head reappeared, mounting. When his left hand came in sight, Grobstock perceived it was grasping the lucky-bag with which a certain philanthropist had started out so joyously that afternoon. The unlucky-bag he felt inclined to dub it now.

"I have recovered it!" observed the *Schnorrer* cheerfully. "As it is written, 'And David recovered all that the Amalekites had taken.' You see in the excitement of the moment I did not notice that you had stolen my packets of silver as well as my salmon. Luckily your cook had not yet removed the fish from the bag — I chid her all the same for neglecting to put it into water, and she opened her mouth not in wisdom. If she had not been a heathen I should have suspected her of trickery, for I knew nothing of the amount of money in the bag, saving your assurance that it did not fall below seventeen shillings, and it would have been easy for her to replace the fish. Therefore, in the words of David, will I give thanks unto Thee, O Lord, among the heathen."

The mental vision of the irruption of Manasseh into the kitchen was not pleasant to Grobstock. However, he only murmured: "How came you to think of it so suddenly?"

"Looking at your clothes reminded me. I was wondering if you had left anything in the pockets."

The donor started — he knew himself a careless rascal — and made as if he would overhaul his garments. The glitter in Manasseh's eye petrified him.

"Do you — do you — mind my looking?" he stammered apologetically.

"Am I a dog?" quoted the *Schnorrer* with dignity. "Am I a thief that you should go over my pockets? If, when I get home," he conceded, commencing to draw distinctions with his thumb, "I should find anything in my pockets that is of no value to anybody but you, do you fear I will not return it? If, on the other hand, I find anything that is of value to me, do you fear I will not keep it?"

"No, but — but — " Grobstock broke down, scarcely grasping the argumentation despite his own clarity of financial insight; he only felt vaguely that the *Schnorrer* was — professionally enough — begging the question.

"But what?" enquired Manasseh. "Surely you need not me to teach you your duty. You cannot be ignorant of the Law of Moses on the point."

"The Law of Moses says nothing on the point!"

"Indeed! What says Deuteronomy? 'When thou reapest thine harvest in thy field, and hast forgot a sheaf in the field, thou shalt not go again to fetch it: it shall be for the stranger, for the fatherless, and for the widow.' Is it not further forbidden to go over the boughs of thy olive-tree again, or to gather the fallen fruit of thy vineyard? You will admit that Moses would have added a prohibition against searching minutely the pockets of cast-off garments, were it not that for forty years our ancestors had to wander in the wilderness in the same clothes, which miraculously waxed with their growth. No, I feel sure you will respect the spirit of the law, for when I went down into your kitchen and examined the door-post to see if you had nailed up a *mezuzah* upon it, knowing that many Jews only flaunt *mezuzahs* on door-posts visible to visitors, it rejoiced me to find one below stairs."

Grobstock's magnanimity responded to the appeal. It would be indeed petty to scrutinise his pockets, or to feel the linings for odd coins. After all he had Manasseh's promise to restore papers and everything of no value.

"Well, well," he said pleasantly, consoled by the thought his troubles had now come to an end — for that day at least — "take them away as they are."

"It is all very well to say take them away," replied Manasseh, with a touch of resentment, "but what am I to take them in?"

"Oh — ah — yes! There must be a sack somewhere — "

"And do you think I would carry them away in a sack? Would you have me look like an old clo' man? I must have a box. I see several in the box-room."

"Very well," said Grobstock resignedly. "If there's an empty one you may have it."

Manasseh laid his stick on the dressing-table and carefully examined the boxes, some of which were carelessly open, while every lock had a key sticking in it. They had travelled far and wide with Grobstock, who invariably combined pleasure with business.

"There is none quite empty," announced the *Schnorrer,* "but in this one there are only a few trifles — a pair of galligaskins and such like — so that if you make me a present of them the box *will* be empty, so far as you are concerned."

"All right," said Grobstock, and actually laughed. The nearer the departure of the *Schnorrer,* the higher his spirits rose.

Manasseh dragged the box towards the bed, and then for the first time since his return from the under-regions, surveyed the medley of garments upon it.

The light-hearted philanthropist, watching his face, saw it instantly change to darkness, like a tropical landscape. His own face grew white. The *Schnorrer* uttered an inarticulate cry, and turned a strange, questioning glance upon his patron.

"What is it now?" faltered Grobstock.

"I miss a pair of pantaloons!"

Grobstock grew whiter. "Nonsense! nonsense!" he muttered.

"I — miss — a — pair — of — pantaloons!" reiterated the *Schnorrer* deliberately.

"Oh, no — you have all I can spare there," said Grobstock uneasily. The *Schnorrer* hastily turned over the heap.

Then his eye flashed fire; he banged his fist on the dressing-table to accompany each *staccato* syllable.

"I — miss — a — pair — of —pan — ta — loons!" he shrieked.

The weak and ductile donor had a bad quarter of a minute.

"Perhaps," he stammered at last, "you — m — mean — the new pair I found had got accidentally mixed up with them."

"Of course I mean the new pair! And so you took them away!

Just because I wasn't looking. I left the room, thinking I had to do with a man of honour. If you had taken an old pair I shouldn't have minded so much; but to rob a poor man of his brand-new breeches!"

"I must have them,' cried Grobstock irascibly. "I have to go to a reception to-morrow, and they are the only pair I shall have to wear. You see I — "

"Oh, very well," interrupted the *Schnorrer*, in low, indifferent tones.

After that there was a dead silence. The *Schnorrer* majestically folded some silk stockings and laid them in the box. Upon them he packed other garments in stern, sorrowful *hauteur*. Grobstock's soul began to tingle with pricks of compunction. Da Costa completed his task, but could not shut the overcrowded box. Grobstock silently seated his weighty person upon the lid. Manasseh neither resented nor welcomed him. When he had turned the key he mutely tilted the sitter off the box and shouldered it with consummate ease. Then he took his staff and strode from the room. Grobstock would have followed him, but the *Schnorrer* waved him back.

"On Friday, then," the conscience-stricken magnate said feebly.

Manasseh did not reply; he slammed the door instead, shutting in the master of the house.

Grobstock fell back on the bed exhausted, looking not unlike the tumbled litter of clothes he replaced. In a minute or two he raised himself and went to the window, and stood watching the sun set behind the trees of the Tenterground. "At any rate I've done with him," he said, and hummed a tune. The sudden bursting open of the door froze it upon his lips. He was almost relieved to find the intruder was only his wife.

"What have you done with Wilkinson?" she cried vehemently. She was a pale, puffy-faced, portly matron, with a permanent air of remembering the exact figure of her dowry.

"With Wilkinson, my dear? Nothing."

"Well, he isn't in the house. I want him, but cook says you've sent him out."

"I? Oh, no," he returned, with dawning uneasiness, looking away from her sceptical gaze.

Suddenly his pupils dilated. A picture from without had painted itself on his retina. It was a picture of Wilkinson —

Wilkinson the austere, Wilkinson the unbending — treading the Tenterground gravel, curved beneath a box! Before him strode the *Schnorrer.*

Never during all his tenure of service in Goodman's Fields had Wilkinson carried anything on his shoulders but his livery. Grobstock would have as soon dreamt of his wife consenting to wear cotton. He rubbed his eyes, but the image persisted.

He clutched at the window curtains to steady himself.

"My Persian curtains!" cried his wife. "What is the matter with you?"

"He must be the Baal Shem himself!" gasped Grobstock unheeding.

"What is it? What are you looking at?"

"N — nothing."

Mrs. Grobstock incredulously approached the window and stared through the panes. She saw Wilkinson in the gardens, but did not recognise him in his new attitude. She concluded that her husband's agitation must have some connection with a beautiful brunette who was tasting the cool of the evening in a sedan chair, and it was with a touch of asperity that she said: "Cook complains of being insulted by a saucy fellow who brought home your fish."

"Oh!" said poor Grobstock. Was he never to be done with the man?

"How came you to send him to her?"

His anger against Manasseh resurged under his wife's peevishness.

"My dear," he cried, "I did not send him anywhere — except to the devil."

"Joseph! You might keep such language for the ears of creatures in sedan chairs."

And Mrs. Grobstock flounced out of the room with a rustle of angry satin.

When Wilkinson reappeared, limp and tired, with his pompousness exuded in perspiration, he sought his master with a message, which he delivered ere the flood of interrogation could burst from Grobstock's lips.

"Mr. da Costa presents his compliments, and says that he has decided on reconsideration not to break his promise to be with you on Friday evening."

"Oh, indeed!", said Grobstock grimly. "And, pray, how came you to carry his box?"

"You told me to, sir!"

"*I* told you!"

"I mean he told me you told me to," said Wilkinson wonderingly. "Didn't you?"

Grobstock hesitated. Since Manasseh *would* be his guest, was it not imprudent to give him away to the livery servant? Besides, he felt a secret pleasure in Wilkinson's humiliation — but for the *Schnorrer* he would never have known that Wilkinson's gold lace concealed a pliable personality. The proverb "Like master like man" did not occur to Grobstock at this juncture.

"I only meant you to carry it to a coach," he murmured.

"He said it was not worth while — the distance was so short."

"Ah! Did you see his house?" enquired Grobstock curiously.

"Yes; a very fine house in Aldgate, with a handsome portico and two stone lions."

Grobstock strove hard not to look surprised.

"I handed the box to the footman."

Grobstock strove harder.

Wilkinson ended with a weak smile: "Would you believe, sir, I thought at first he brought home your fish! He dresses so peculiarly. He must be an original."

"Yes, yes; an eccentric like Baron D'Aguilar, whom he visits," said Grobstock eagerly. He wondered, indeed, whether he was not speaking the truth. Could he have been the victim of a practical joke, a prank? Did not a natural aristocracy ooze from every pore of his mysterious visitor? Was not every tone, every gesture, that of a man born to rule? "You must remember, too," he added, "that he is a Spaniard."

"Ah, I see," said Wilkinson in profound accents.

"I daresay he dresses like everybody else, though, when he dines or sups out," Grobstock added lightly. "I only brought him in by accident. But go to your mistress! She wants you."

"Yes, sir. Oh, by the way, I forgot to tell you he hopes you will save him a slice of his salmon."

"Go to your mistress!"

"You did not tell me a Spanish nobleman was coming to us on Friday," said his spouse later in the evening.

"No," he admitted curtly.

But is he?"

"No — at least, not a nobleman."

"What then? I have to learn about my guests from my servants."

"Apparently."

"Oh! and you think that's right!"

"To gossip with your servants? Certainly not."

"If my husband will not tell me anything — if he has only
eyes for sedan chairs."

Joseph thought it best to kiss Mrs. Grobstock.

"A fellow-Director, I suppose?" she urged, more mildly.

"A fellow-Israelite. He has promised to come at six."

Manasseh was punctual to the second. Wilkinson ushered
him in. The hostess had robed herself in her best to do honour
to a situation which her husband awaited with what hope he
could. She looked radiant in a gown of blue silk; her hair was
done in a tuft and round her neck was an "esclavage," consisting
of festoons of gold chains. The Sabbath table was equally festive
with its ponderous silver candelabra, coffee-urn, and consecration
cup, its flower-vases, and fruit-salvers. The dining-room itself was
a handsome apartment; its buffets glittered with Venetian glass
and Dresden porcelain, and here and there gilt pedestals supported globes of gold and silver fish.

At the first glance at his guest, Grobstock's blood ran cold.

Manasseh had not turned a hair, nor changed a single gar-
ment. At the next glance Grobstock's blood boiled. A second
figure loomed in Manasseh's wake — a short *Schnorrer*, even dingier than da Costa, and with none of his dignity, a clumsy,
stooping *Schnorrer*, with a cajoling grin on his mud-coloured,
hairy face. Neither removed his headgear.

Mrs. Grobstock remained glued to her chair in astonishment.

"Peace be unto you," said the King of *Schnorrers*, "I have
brought with me my friend Yankelé ben Yitzchok of whom I
told you."

Yankelé nodded, grinning harder than ever.

"You never told me he was coming," Grobstock rejoined, with
an apoplectic air.

"Did I not tell you that he always supped with me on Friday
evenings?" Manasseh reminded him quietly. "It is so good of

him to accompany me even here — he will make the necessary third at grace."

The host took a frantic surreptitious glance at his wife. It was evident that her brain was in a whirl, the evidence of her senses conflicting with vague doubts of the possibilities of Spanish grandeeism and with a lingering belief in her husband's sanity.

Grobstock resolved to snatch the benefit of her doubts. "My dear," said he, "this is Mr. da Costa."

"Manasseh Bueno Barzillai Azevedo da Costa," said the *Schnorrer*.

The dame seemed a whit startled and impressed. She bowed, but words of welcome were still congealed in her throat.

"And this is Yankelé ben Yitzchok," added Manasseh. "A poor friend of mine. I do not doubt, Mrs. Grobstock, that as a pious woman, the daughter of Moses Bernberg (his memory for a blessing), you prefer grace with three."

"Any friend of yours is welcome!" She found her lips murmuring the conventional phrase without being able to check their output.

"I never doubted that either," said Manasseh gracefully. "Is not the hospitality of Moses Bernberg's beautiful daughter a proverb?"

Moses Bernberg's daughter could not deny this; her salon was the rendezvous of rich bagmen, brokers and bankers, tempered by occasional young bloods and old bucks not of the Jewish faith (nor any other). But she had never before encountered a personage so magnificently shabby, nor extended her proverbial hospitality to a Polish *Schnorrer* uncompromisingly musty. Joseph did not dare meet her eye.

"Sit down there, Yankelé," he said hurriedly, in ghastly genial accents, and he indicated a chair at the farthest possible point from the hostess. He placed Manasseh next to his Polish parasite, and seated himself as a buffer between his guests and his wife. He was burning with inward indignation at the futile rifling of his wardrobe, but he dared not say anything in the hearing of his spouse.

"It is a beautiful custom, this of the Sabbath guest, is it not, Mrs. Grobstock?" remarked Manasseh as he took his seat. "I never neglect it — even when I go out to the Sabbath-meal as to-night."

The late Miss Bernberg was suddenly reminded of auld lang syne: her father (who according to a wag of the period had divided his time between the Law and the profits) having been a depositary of ancient tradition. Perhaps these obsolescent customs, unsuited to prosperous times, had lingered longer among the Spanish grandees. She seized an early opportunity, when the Sephardic *Schnorrer* was taking his coffee from Wilkinson, of putting the question to her husband, who fell in weakly with her illusions. He knew there was no danger of Manasseh's beggarly status leaking out; no expressions of gratitude were likely to fall from that gentleman's lips. He even hinted that da Costa dressed so fussily to keep his poor friend in countenance. Nevertheless, Mrs. Grobstock, while not without admiration for the Quixotism, was not without resentment for being dragged into it. She felt that such charity should begin and end at home.

"I see you did save me a slice of salmon," said Manasseh, manipulating his fish.

"What salmon was that?" asked the hostess, pricking up her ears.

"One I had from Mr. da Costa on Wednesday," said the host.

"Oh, that! It was delicious. I am sure it was very kind of you, Mr. da Costa, to make us such a nice present," said the hostess, her resentment diminishing. "We had company last night, and everybody praised it till none was left. This is another, but I hope it is to your liking," she finished anxiously.

"Yes, it's very fair, very fair, indeed. I don't know when I've tasted better, except at the house of the President of the *Deputados*. But Yankelé here is a connoisseur in fish, not easy to please. What say you, Yankelé?"

Yankelé munched a muffled approval.

"Help yourself to more bread and butter, Yankelé," said Manasseh. "Make yourself at home — remember you're my guest." Silently he added: "The other fork!"

Grobstock's irritation found vent in a complaint that the salad wanted vinegar.

"How can you say so? It's perfect," said Mrs. Grobstock "Salad is cook's speciality."

Manasseh tasted it critically. "On salads you must come to me," he said. "It does not want vinegar," was his verdict; "but a little more oil would certainly improve it. Oh, there is no one dresses salad like Hyman!"

Hyman's fame as the *Kosher chef* who superintended the big dinners at the London Tavern had reached Mrs. Grobstock's ears, and she was proportionately impressed.

"They say his pastry is so good," she observed, to be in the running.

"Yes," said Manasseh, "in kneading and puffing he stands alone."

"Our cook's tarts are quite as nice," said Grobstock roughly.

"We shall see," Manasseh replied guardedly. "Though, as for almond-cakes, Hyman himself makes none better than I get from my cousin, Barzillai of Fenchurch Street."

"Your cousin!" exclaimed Grobstock, "the West Indian merchant!"

"The same — formerly of Barbadoes. Still, your cook knows how to make coffee, though I can tell you do not get it direct from the plantation like the wardens of my Synagogue."

Grobstock was once again piqued with curiosity as to the *Schnorrer's* identity.

"You accuse me of having stone figures in my house," he said boldly, "but what about the lions in front of yours?"

"I have no lions," said Manasseh.

"Wilkinson told me so. Didn't you, Wilkinson?"

"Wilkinson is a slanderer. That was the house of Nathaniel Furtado."

Grobstock began to choke with chagrin. He perceived at once that the *Schnorrer* had merely had the clothes conveyed direct to the house of a wealthy private dealer.

"Take care!" exclaimed the *Schnorrer* anxiously, "you are spluttering sauce all over that waistcoat, without any consideration for me."

Joseph suppressed himself with an effort. Open discussion would betray matters to his wife, and he was now too deeply enmeshed in falsehoods by default. But he managed to whisper angrily, "Why did you tell Wilkinson I ordered him to carry your box?"

"To save your credit in his eyes. How was he to know we had quarrelled? He would have thought you discourteous to your guest."

"That's all very fine. But why did you sell my clothes?"

"You did not expect me to wear them? No, I know my station, thank God."

"What is that you are saying, Mr. da Costa?" asked the hostess.

"Oh, we are talking of Dan Mendoza," replied Grobstock glibly; "wondering if he'll beat Dick Humphreys at Doncaster."

"Oh, Joseph, didn't you have enough of Dan Mendoza at supper last night?" protested his wife.

"It is not a subject *I* ever talk about," said the *Schnorrer,* fixing his host with a reproachful glance.

Grobstock desperately touched his foot under the table, knowing he was selling his soul to the King of *Schnorrers,* but too flaccid to face the moment.

"No, da Costa doesn't usually," he admitted. "Only Dan Mendoza being a Portuguese I happened to ask if he was ever seen in the Synagogue."

"If I had my way," growled da Costa, "he should be excommunicated — a bruiser, a defacer of God's image!"

"By gad, no!" cried Grobstock, stirred up. "If you had seen him lick the Badger in thirty-five minutes on a twenty-four foot stage — "

"Joseph! Joseph! Remember it is the Sabbath!" cried Mrs. Grobstock.

"I would willingly exchange our Dan Mendoza for your David Levi," said da Costa severely.

David Levi was the literary ornament of the Ghetto; a shoemaker and hat-dresser who cultivated Hebrew philology and the Muses, and broke a lance in defence of his creed with Dr. Priestley, the discoverer of Oxygen, and Tom Paine, the discoverer of Reason.

"Pshaw! David Levi! The mad hatter!" cried Grobstock. "He makes nothing at all out of his books."

"You should subscribe for more copies," retorted Manasseh.

"I would if you wrote them," rejoined Grobstock, with a grimace.

"I got six copies of his *Lingua Sacra,*" Manasseh declared with dignity, "and a dozen of his translation of the Pentateuch."

"You can afford it!" snarled Grobstock, with grim humour. "I have to earn my money."

"It is very good of Mr. da Costa, all the same," interposed the hostess. "How many men, born to great possessions, remain quite indifferent to learning!"

"True, most true," said da Costa. "Men-of-the-Earth, most of them."

After supper he trolled the Hebrew grace hilariously, assisted by Yankelé, and ere he left he said to the hostess, "May the Lord bless you with children!"

"Thank you," she answered, much moved.

"You see I should be so pleased to marry your daughter if you had one."

"You are very complimentary," she murmured, but her husband's exclamation drowned hers, "You marry my daughter!"

"Who else moves among better circles — would be more easily able to find her a suitable match?"

"Oh, in *that* sense," said Grobstock, mollified in one direction, irritated in another.

"In what other sense? You do not think I, a Sephardi, would marry her myself!"

"My daughter does not need your assistance,'" replied Grobstock shortly.

"Not yet," admitted Manasseh, rising to go; "but when the time comes, where will you find a better marriage broker? I have had a finger in the marriage of greater men's daughters. You see, when I recommend a maiden or a young man it is from no surface knowledge. I have seen them in the intimacy of their homes—above all I am able to say whether they are of a good, charitable disposition. Good Sabbath!"

"Good Sabbath," murmured the host and hostess in farewell. Mrs. Grobstock thought he need not be above shaking hands, for all his grand acquaintances.

"This way, Yankelé," said Manasseh, showing him to the door. "I am so glad you were able to come — you must come again."

CHAPTER III

SHOWING HOW HIS MAJESTY WENT TO THE THEATRE
AND WAS WOOED

As Manasseh the Great, first beggar in Europe, sauntered across Goodman's Fields, attended by his Polish parasite, both serenely digesting the supper provided by the Treasurer of the Great Synagogue, Joseph Grobstock, a martial music clove suddenly the quiet evening air, and set the *Schnorrers'* pulses bounding. From the Tenterground emerged a squad of recruits, picturesque in white fatigue dress, against which the mounted officers showed gallant in blue surtouts and scarlet-striped trousers.

"Ah!" said da Costa, with swelling breast. "There go my soldiers!"

"Your soldiers!" ejaculated Yankelé in astonishment.

"Yes — do you not see they are returning to the India House in Leadenhall Street?"

"And vat of dat?" said Yankelé, shrugging his shoulders and spreading out his palms.

"What of that? Surely you have not forgotten that the clodpate at whose house I have just entertained you is a Director of the East India Company, whose soldiers these are?"

"Oh," said Yankelé, his mystified face relaxing in a smile. The smile fled before the stern look in the Spaniard's eyes; he hastened to conceal his amusement. Yankelé was by nature a droll, and it cost him a good deal to take his patron as seriously as that potentate took himself. Perhaps if Manasseh Bueno Barzillai Azevedo da Costa had had more humour he would have had less momentum. Your man of action is blind in one eye. Cæsar would not have come and conquered if he had really seen.

Wounded by that temporary twinkle in his client's eye, the patron moved on silently, in step with the military air.

"It is a beautiful night," observed Yankelé in contrition. The words had hardly passed his lips before he became conscious that he had spoken the truth. The moon was peeping from behind a white cloud, and the air was soft, and broken shadows of foliage lay across the path, and the music was a song of love and bravery. Somehow, Yankelé began to think of da Costa's lovely daughter. Her face floated in the moonlight.

Manasseh shrugged his shoulders, unappeased.

"When one has supped well, it is always a beautiful night," he said testily. It was as if the cloud had overspread the moon, and a thick veil had fallen over the face of da Costa's lovely daughter. But Yankelé recovered himself quickly.

"Ah, yes," he said, "you have indeed made it a beautiful night for me."

The King of *Schnorrers* waved his staff deprecatingly.

"It is always a beautiful night ven I am mid *you*," added Yankelé, undaunted.

"It is strange," replied Manasseh musingly, "that I should have admitted to my hearth and Grobstock's table one who is, after all, but a half-brother in Israel."

"But Grobstock is also a Tedesco," protested Yankelé.

"That is also what I wonder at," rejoined da Costa. "I cannot make out how I have come to be so familiar with him."

"You see!" ventured the Tedesco timidly. "P'raps ven Grobstock had really had a girl you might even have come to marry her."

"Guard your tongue! A Sephardi cannot marry a Tedesco! It would be a degradation."

"Yes—but de oder vay round. A Tedesco *can* marry a Sephardi, not so? Dat is a rise. If Grobstock's daughter had married you, she vould have married above her," he ended, with an ingenuous air.

"True," admitted Manasseh. "But then, as Grobstock's daughter does not exist, and my wife does—!"

"Ah, but if you vas me," said Yankelé, "vould you rader marry a Tedesco or a Sephardi?"

"A Sephardi, of course. But — "

"I vill be guided by you," interrupted the Pole hastily. "You be de visest man I have ever known."

"But — " Manasseh repeated.

"Do not deny it. You be! Instantly vill I seek out a Sephardi maiden and ved her. P'raps you crown your counsel by choosing von for me. Vat?"

Manasseh was visibly mollified.

"How do I know your taste?" he asked hesitatingly.

"Oh, any Spanish girl would be a prize," replied Yankelé. "Even ven she had a face like a Passover cake. But still I prefer a Pentecost blossom."

"What kind of beauty do you like best?"

"Your daughter's style," plumply answered the Pole.

"But there are not many like that," said da Costa unsuspiciously.

"No — she is like de Rose of Sharon. But den dere are not many handsome faders."

Manasseh bethought himself. "There is Gabriel, the corpse-watcher's daughter. People consider his figure and deportment good."

"Pooh! Offal! She's ugly enough to keep de Messiah from coming. Vy, she's like cut out of de fader's face! Besides, consider his occupation! You vould not advise dat I marry into such a low family! Be you not my benefactor?"

"Well, but I cannot think of any good-looking girl that would be suitable."

Yankelé looked at him with a roguish, insinuating smile. "Say not dat! Have you not told Grobstock you be de first of marriage-brokers?"

But Manasseh shook his head.

"No, you be quite right," said Yankelé humbly; "I could not get a really beaudiful girl unless I married your Deborah herself."

"No, I am afraid not," said Manasseh sympathetically.

Yankelé took the plunge.

"Ah, vy can I not hope to call you fader-in-law?"

Manasseh's face was contorted by a spasm of astonishment and indignation. He came to a standstill.

"Dat must be a fine piece," said Yankelé quickly, indicating a flamboyant picture of a fearsome phantom hovering over a sombre moat.

They had arrived at Leman Street, and had stopped before Goodman's Fields Theatre. Manasseh's brow cleared.

"It is *The Castle Spectre*," he said graciously. "Would you like to see it?"

"But it is half over — "

"Oh, no," said da Costa, scanning the play bill. "There was a farce by O'Keefe to start with. The night is yet young. The drama will be just beginning."

"But it is de Sabbath — ve must not pay."

Manasseh's brow clouded again in wrathful righteous surprise. "Did you think I was going to pay?" he gasped.

"N-n-no," stammered the Pole, abashed. "But you haven't got no orders?"

"Orders? Me? Will you do me the pleasure of accepting a seat in my box?"

"In your box?"

"Yes, there is plenty of room. Come this way," said Manasseh. "I haven't been to the play myself for over a year. I am too busy always. It will be an agreeable change."

Yankelé hung back, bewildered.

"Through this door," said Manasseh encouragingly. "Come — you shall lead the way."

"But dey vill not admit me!"

"Will not admit you! When I give you a seat in my box! Are you mad? Now you shall just go in without me — I insist upon it. I will show you Manasseh Bueno Barzillai Azevedo da Costa is a man whose word is the Law of Moses; true as the Talmud. Walk straight through the portico, and, if the attendant endeavours to stop you, simply tell him Mr. da Costa has given you a seat in his box."

Not daring to exhibit scepticism — nay, almost confident in the powers of his extraordinary protector, Yankelé put his foot on the threshold of the lobby.

"But you be coming, too?" he said, turning back.

"Oh, yes, I don't intend to miss the performance. Have no fear."

Yankelé walked boldly ahead, and brushed by the doorkeeper of the little theatre without appearing conscious of him; indeed, the official was almost impressed into letting the *Schnorrer* pass unquestioned as one who had gone out between the acts. But the visitor was too dingy for anything but the stage-door — he had the air of those nondescript beings who hang mysteriously about the hinder recesses of playhouses. Recovering himself just in time, the functionary (a meek little Cockney) hailed the intruder with a backward-drawing "Hi!"

"Vat you vant?" said Yankelé, turning his head.

"Vhere's your ticket?"

"Don't vant no ticket."

"Don't you? I does," rejoined the little man, who was a humorist.

"Mr. da Costa has given me a seat in his box."

"Oh, indeed! You'd swear to that in the box?"

"By my head. He gave it me."

"A seat in his box?"

"Yes."

"Mr. da Costa, you vos a-sayin', I think?"

"The same."

"Ah! this vay, then!"

And the humorist pointed to the street.

Yankelé did not budge.

"This vay, my lud!" cried the little humorist peremptorily.

"I tells you I'm going into Mr. da Costa's box!"

"And I tells you you're a-goin' into the gutter." And the official seized him by the scruff of the neck and began pushing him forwards with his knee.

"Now then! what's this?"

A stern, angry voice broke like a thunderclap upon the humorist's ears. He released his hold of the *Schnorrer* and looked up, to behold a strange, shabby, stalwart figure towering over him in censorious majesty.

"Why are you hustling this poor man?" demanded Manasseh.

"He wanted to sneak in," the little Cockney replied, half apologetically, half resentfully. "Expect 'e 'ails from Saffron 'Ill, and 'as 'is eye on the vipes. Told me some gammon — a cock-and-bull story about having a seat in a box."

"In Mr. da Costa's box, I suppose?" said Manasseh, ominously calm, with a menacing glitter in his eye.

"Ye-es," said the humorist, astonished and vaguely alarmed. Then the storm burst.

"You impertinent scoundrel! You jackanapes! You low, beggarly rapscallion! And so you refused to show my guest into my box!"

"Are you Mr. da Costa?" faltered the humorist.

"Yes, *I* am Mr. da Costa, but *you* won't much longer be door-keeper, if this is the way you treat people who come to see your pieces. Because, forsooth, the man looks poor, you think you can bully him safely — forgive me, Yankelé, I am so sorry I did not manage to come here before you, and spare you this insulting treatment! And as for you, my fine fellow, let me tell you that you make a great mistake in judging from appearances. There are some good friends of mine who could buy up your theatre and you and your miserable little soul at a moment's notice, and to look at them you would think they were cadgers. One of these days — hark you! — you will kick out a person of quality, and be kicked out yourself."

"I — I'm very sorry, sir."

"Don't say that to me. It is my guest you owe an apology to. Yes — and, by Heaven! You shall pay it, though he is no plutocrat, but only what he appears. Surely, because I wish to give a treat to a poor man who has, perhaps, never been to the play in his life, I am not bound to send him to the gallery — I can give him a corner in my box if I choose. There is no rule against that, I presume?"

"No, sir, I can't say as there is," said the humorist humbly. "But you will allow, sir, it's rayther unusual."

"Unusual! Of course, it's unusual. Kindness and consideration for the poor are always unusual. The poor are trodden upon at every opportunity, treated like dogs, not men. If I had invited a drunken fop, you'd have met him hat in hand (no, no, you needn't take it off to me now; it's too late). But a sober, poor man — by gad! I shall report your incivility to the management, and you'll be lucky if I don't thrash you with this stick into the bargain."

"But 'ow vos I to know, sir?"

"Don't speak to me, I tell you. If you have anything to urge in extenuation of your disgraceful behaviour, address your remarks to my guest."

"You'll overlook it this time, sir," said the little humorist, turning to Yankelé.

"Next time, p'raps, you believe me ven I say I have a seat in Mr. da Costa's box," replied Yankelé, in gentle reproach.

"Well, if *you're* satisfied, Yankelé," said Manasseh, with a touch of scorn, "I have no more to say. Go along, my man, show us to our box."

The official bowed and led them into the corridor. Suddenly he turned back.

"What box is it, please?" he said timidly.

"Blockhead!" cried Manasseh. "Which box should it be? The empty one, of course."

"But, sir, there are two boxes empty," urged the poor humorist deprecatingly, "the stage-box and the one by the gallery."

"Dolt! Do I look the sort of person who is content with a box on the ceiling? Go back to your post, sir — I'll find the box myself — Heaven send you wisdom — go back, some one might sneak in while you are away, and it would just serve you right."

The little man slunk back half dazed, glad to escape from this overwhelming personality, and in a few seconds Manasseh stalked into the empty box, followed by Yankelé, whose mouth was a grin and whose eye a twinkle. As the Spaniard took his seat there was a slight outburt of clapping and stamping from a house impatient for the end of the *entr'acte*.

Manasseh craned his head over the box to see the house, which in turned craned to see him, glad of any diversion, and some people, imagining the applause had reference to the new-comer, whose head appeared to be that of a foreigner of distinction, joined in it. The contagion spread, and in a minute Manasseh was the cynosure of all eyes and the unmistakable recipient of an "ovation." He bowed twice or thrice in unruffled dignity.

There were some who recognised him, but they joined in the reception with wondering amusement. Not a few, indeed, of the audience were Jews, for Goodman's Fields was the Ghetto Theatre, and the Sabbath was not a sufficient deterrent to a lax generation. The audiences — mainly German and Poles — came to the little unfashionable playhouse as one happy family. Distinctions of rank were trivial, and gallery held converse with circle, and pit collogued with box. Supper parties were held on the benches.

In a box that gave on the pit a portly Jewess sat stiffly, arrayed in the very pink of fashion, in a spangled robe of India muslin, with a diamond necklace and crescent, her head crowned by terraces of curls and flowers.

"Betsy!" called up a jovial feminine voice from the pit, when the applause had subsided.

"Betsy" did not move, but her cheeks grew hot and red. She had got on in the world, and did not care to recognise her old crony.

"Betsy!" iterated the well-meaning woman. "By your life and mine, you must taste a piece of my fried fish." And she held up a slice of cold plaice, beautifully browned.

Betsy drew back, striving unsuccessfully to look unconscious. To her relief the curtain rose, and *The Castle Spectre* walked. Yankelé, who had scarcely seen anything but private theatricals, representing the discomfiture of the wicked Haman and the triumph of Queen Esther (a *rôle* he had once played himself in his mother's old clothes), was delighted with the thrills and terrors of the ghostly melodrama. It was not till the conclusion of the second act that the emotion the beautiful but injured heroine cost him welled over again into matrimonial speech.

"Ve vind up de night glorious," he said.

"I am glad you like it. It is certainly an enjoyable performance," Manasseh answered with stately satisfaction.

"Your daughter, Deborah," Yankelé ventured timidly, "do she ever go to de play?"

"No, I do not take my womankind about. Their duty lies at home. As it is written, I call my wife not 'wife' but 'home.' "

"But dink how dey vould enjoy deirselves!"

"We are not sent here to enjoy ourselves."

"True — most true," said Yankelé, pulling a smug face. "Ve be sent here to obey de Law of Moses. But do not remind me I be a sinner in Israel."

"How so?"

"I am twenty-five — yet I have no vife."

"I daresay you had plenty in Poland."

"By my soul, not. Only von, and her I gave *gett* (divorce) for barrenness. You can write to de Rabbi of my town."

"Why should I write? It's not my affair."

"But I vant it to be your affair."

Manasseh glared. "Do you begin that again?" he murmured.

"It is not so much dat I desire your daughter for a vife as you for a fader-in-law."

"It cannot be!" said Manasseh more gently.

"Oh dat I had been born a Sephardi!" said Yankelé with a hopeless groan.

"It is too late now," said da Costa soothingly.

"Dey say it's never too late to mend," moaned the Pole. "Is dere no vay for me to be converted to Spanish Judaism? I could easily pronounce Hebrew in your superior vay."

"Our Judaism differs in no essential respect from yours — it is a question of blood. You cannot change your blood. As it is said, 'And the blood is the life.' "

"I know, I know dat I aspire too high. Oh, vy did you become my friend, vy did you make me believe you cared for me — so dat I tink of you day and night — and now, ven I ask you to be my fader-in-law, you say it cannot be. It is like a knife in de heart! Tink how proud and happy I should be to call you my fader-in-law. All my life vould be devoted to you — my von thought to be vordy of such a man."

"You are not the first I have been compelled to refuse," said Manasseh, with emotion.

"Vat helps me dat dere be other *Schlemihls* (unlucky persons)?" quoted Yankelé, with a sob. "How can I live midout you for a fader-in-law?"

"I am sorry for you — more sorry than I have ever been."

"Den you do care for me! I vill not give up hope. I vill not take no for no answer. Vat is dis blood dat it should divide Jew from Jew, dat it should prevent me becoming de son-in-law of de only man I have ever loved? Say not so. Let me ask you again — in a month or a year — even twelve months vould I vait, ven you vould only promise not to pledge yourself to anoder man."

"But if I became your father-in-law — mind, I only say if — not only would I not keep you, but you would have to keep my Deborah."

"And supposing?"

"But you are not able to keep a wife!"

"Not able? Who told you dat?" cried Yankelé indignantly.

"You yourself! Why, when I first befriended you, you told me you were blood-poor."

"Dat I told you as a *Schnorrer*. But now I speak to you as a suitor."

"True," admitted Manasseh, instantly appreciating the distinction.

"And as a suitor I tell you I can *schnorr* enough to keep two vives."

"But do you tell this to da Costa the father or da Costa the marriage-broker?"

"Hush!" from all parts of the house as the curtain went up and the house settled down. But Yankelé was no longer in *rapport* with the play; the spectre had ceased to thrill and the heroine to touch. His mind was busy with feverish calculations of income, scraping together every penny he could raise by hook or crook. He even drew out a crumpled piece of paper and a pencil, but thrust them back into his pocket when he saw Manasseh's eye.

"I forgot," he murmured apologetically. "Being at de play made me forget it was de Sabbath." And he pursued his calculations mentally, this being naturally less work.

When the play was over the two beggars walked out into the cool night air.

"I find," Yankelé began eagerly in the vestibule, "I make at least von hundred and fifty pounds" — he paused to acknowledge the farewell salutation of the little door-keeper at his elbow — "a hundred and fifty a year."

"Indeed!" said Manasseh, in respectful astonishment.

"Yes! I have reckoned it all up. Ten are de sources of charity —"

"As it is written," interrupted Manasseh with unction, " 'With ten sayings was the world created; there were ten generations from Noah to Abraham; with ten trials our father Abraham was tried; ten miracles were wrought for our fathers in Egypt and ten at the Red Sea; and ten things were created on the eve of the Sabbath in the twilight!' And now it shall be added, 'Ten good deeds the poor man affords the rich man.' Proceed, Yankelé."

"First comes my allowance from de Synagogue — eight pounds. Vonce a veek I call and receive half-a-crown."

"Is that all? Our Synagogue allows three-and-six."

"Ah!" sighed the Pole wistfully. "Did I not say you be a superior race?"

"But that only makes six pound ten!"

"I know — de oder tirty shillings I allow for Passover cakes and groceries. Den for Synagogue-knocking I get ten guin —"

"Stop! stop!" cried Manasseh, with a sudden scruple. "Ought I to listen to financial details on the Sabbath?"

"Certainly, ven dey be connected vid my marriage — vich is a Commandment. It is de Law ve really discuss."

"You are right. Go on, then. But remember, even if you can prove you can *schnorr* enough to keep a wife, I do not bind myself to consent."

"You be already a fader to me — vy vill you not be a fader-in-law? Anyhow, you vill find me a fader-in-law," he added hastily, seeing the blackness gathering again on da Costa's brow.

"Nay, nay, we must not talk of business on the Sabbath," said Manasseh evasively. "Proceed with your statement of income."

"Ten guineas for Synagogue-knocking. I have twenty clients who —"

"Stop a minute! I cannot pass that item."

"Vy not? It is true."

"Maybe! But Synagogue-knocking is distinctly *work!*"

"Vork?"

"Well, if going round early in the morning to knock at the doors of twenty pious persons, and rouse them for morning service, isn't work, then the Christian bell-ringer is a beggar. No, no! Profits from this source I cannot regard as legitimate."

"But most *Schnorrers* be Synagogue-knockers!"

"Most *Schnorrers* are Congregation-men or Psalms-men," retorted the Spaniard witheringly. "But I call it debasing. What! To assist at the services for a fee! To worship one's Maker for hire! Under such conditions to pray is to work." His breast swelled with majesty and scorn.

"I cannot call it vork," protested the *Schnorrer*. "Vy at dat rate you vould make out dat de minister vorks? or de preacher? Vy, I reckon fourteen pounds a year to my services as Congregation-man."

"Fourteen pounds! As much as that?"

"Yes, you see dere's my private customers as vell as de Synagogue. Ven dere is mourning in a house dey cannot alvays get together ten friends for de services, so I make von. How can you call that vork? It is friendship. And the more dey pay me de more friendship I feel," asserted Yankelé with a twinkle. "Den de Synagogue allows me a little extra for announcing de dead."

In those primitive times, when a Jewish newspaper was undreamt of, the day's obituary was published by a peripatetic *Schnorrer,* who went about the Ghetto rattling a pyx — a copper money-box with a handle and a lid closed by a padlock. On hearing this death-rattle, anyone who felt curious would ask the *Schnorrer:*

"Who's dead to-day?"

"So-and-so ben So-and-so — funeral on such a day — mourning service at such an hour," the *Schnorrer* would reply, and the enquirer would piously put something into the "byx," as it was called. The collection was handed over to the Holy Society — in other words, the Burial Society.

"P'raps you call that vork?" concluded Yankelé, in timid challenge.

"Of course I do. What do you call it?"

"Valking exercise. It keeps me healty. Vonce von of my customers (from whom I *schnorred* half-a-crown a veek) said he was tired of my coming and getting it every Friday. He vanted to compound mid me for six pound a year, but I vouldn't."

"But it was a very fair offer. He only deducted ten shillings for the interest on his money."

"Dat I didn't mind. But I wanted a pound more for his depriving me of my valking exercise, and dat he vouldn't pay, so he goes on giving me de half-crown a veek. Some of dese charitable persons are terribly mean. But vat I vant to say is dat I carry de byx mostly in the streets vere my customers lay, and it gives me more standing as a *Schnorrer.*"

"No, no, that is a delusion. What! Are you weak-minded enough to believe that? All the philanthropists say so, of course, but surely you know that *schnorring* and work should never be mixed. A man cannot do two things properly. He must choose his profession, and stick to it. A friend of mine once succumbed to the advice of the philanthropists instead of asking mine. He had one of the best provincial rounds in the kingdom, but in every town he weakly listened to the lectures of the president of the congregation inculcating work, and at last he actually invested the savings of years in jewellery, and went round trying to peddle it. The presidents all bought something to encourage him (though they beat down the price so that there was no profit in it), and they all expressed their pleasure at his working for his living, and showing a manly independence. 'But I *schnorr* also,' he reminded them, holding out his hand when they had finished. It was in vain. No one gave him a farthing. He had blundered beyond redemption. At one blow he had destroyed one of the most profitable connections a *Schnorrer* ever had, and without even getting anything for the goodwill. So if you will be guided by me, Yankelé, you will do nothing to assist the philanthropists to keep you. It destroys their satisfaction. A *Schnorrer* cannot be too careful. And once you begin to work, where are you to draw the line?"

"But you be a marriage-broker yourself," said Yankelé imprudently.

"That!" thundered Manasseh angrily, "That is not work! That is pleasure!"

"Vy look! Dere is Hennery Simons," cried Yankelé, hoping to divert his attention. But he only made matters worse.

Henry Simons was a character variously known as the Tumbling Jew, Harry the Dancer, and the Juggling Jew. He was afterwards to become famous as the hero of a slander case which deluged England with pamphlets for and against, but for the present he had merely outraged the feelings of his fellow *Schnorrers* by budding out in a direction so rare as to suggest preliminary baptism. He stood now playing antic and sleight-of-hand tricks — surrounded by a crowd — a curious figure crowned by a velvet skull-cap from which wisps of hair protruded, with a scarlet handkerchief thrust through his girdle. His face was an olive oval, bordered by ragged tufts of beard and stamped with melancholy.

You see the results of working," cried Manasseh. "It brings temptation to work on Sabbath. That Epicurean there is profaning the Holy Day. Come away! A *Schnorrer* is far more certain of The-World-To-Come. No, decidedly, I will not give my daughter to a worker, or to a *Schnorrer* who makes illegitimate profits."

"But I *make* de profits all de same," persisted Yankelé.

"You make them to-day — but to-morrow? There is no certainty about them. Work of whatever kind is by its very nature unreliable. At any moment trade may be slack. People may become less pious, and you lose your Synagogue-knocking. Or more pious — and they won't want congregation-men."

"But new Synagogues spring up," urged Yankelé.

"New Synagogues are full of enthusiasm," retorted Manasseh. "The members are their own congregation-men."

Yankelé had his roguish twinkle. "At first," he admitted, "but de *Schnorrer* vaits his time."

Manasseh shook his head. "*Schnorring* is the only occupation that is regular all the year round," he said. "Everything else may fail — the greatest commercial houses may totter to the ground; as it is written, 'He humbleth the proud.' But the *Schnorrer* is always secure. Whoever falls, there are always enough left to look after *him*. If you were a father, Yankelé, you would understand my feelings. How can a man allow his daughter's future happiness to repose on a basis so uncertain as work? No, no. What do you make by your district visiting? Everything turns on that."

"Twenty-five shilling a veek!"

"Really?"

"Law of Moses! In sixpences, shillings, and half-crowns. Vy in Houndsditch alone, I have two streets all except a few houses."

"But are they safe? Population shifts. Good streets go down."

"Dat twenty-five shillings is as safe as Mocatta's business. I have it all written down at home — you can inspect de books if you choose."

"No, no," said Manasseh, with a grand wave of his stick. "If I did not believe you, I should not entertain your proposal for a moment. It rejoices me exceedingly to find you have devoted so much attention to this branch. I always held strongly that the rich should be visited in their own homes, and I grieve to see this personal touch, this contact with the very people to whom you give the good deeds, being replaced by lifeless circulars. One owes it to one's position in life to afford the wealthy classes the opportunity of charity warm from the heart; they should not be neglected and driven in their turn to write cheques in cold blood, losing all that human sympathy which comes from personal intercourse — as it is written, 'Charity delivers from death.' But do you think charity that is given publicly through a secretary and advertised in annual reports has so great a redeeming power as that slipped privately into the hands of the poor man, who makes a point of keeping secret from every donor what he has received from the others?"

"I am glad you don't call collecting de money vork," said Yankelé, with a touch of sarcasm which was lost on da Costa.

"No, so long as the donor can't show any 'value received' in return. And there's more friendship in *such* a call, Yankelé, than in going to a house of mourning to pray for a fee."

"Oh," said Yankelé, wincing. "Den p'raps you strike out all my Year-Time item!"

"Year-Time! What's that?"

"Don't you know?" said the Pole, astonished. "Ven a man has Year-Time, he feels charitable for de day."

"Do you mean when he commemorates the anniversary of the death of one of his family? We Sephardim call that 'making years'! But are there enough Year-Times, as you call them, in your Synagogue?"

"Dere might be more—I only make about fifteen pounds. Our colony is, as you say, too new. De Globe Road Cemetery is as empty as a Synagogue on veek-days. De faders have left *deir* faders on de Continent, and kept many Year-Times out of de country. But in a few years many faders and moders must die off here, and every parent leaves two or tree sons to have Year-Times, and every child two or tree broders and a fader. Den every day more German Jews come here — vich means more and more to die. I tink indeed it vould be fair to double this item."

"No, no; stick to facts. It is an iniquity to speculate in the misfortunes of our fellow-creatures."

"Somebody must die dat I may live," retorted Yankelé roguishly; "de vorld is so created. Did you not quote, 'Charity delivers from death'? If people lived for ever, *Schnorrers* could not live at all."

"Hush! The world could not exist without *Schnorrers*. As it is written, 'And Repentance and *Prayer* and CHARITY avert the evil decree.' Charity is put last — it is the climax — the greatest thing on earth. And the *Schnorrer* is the greatest man on earth; for it stands in the Talmud, 'He who causes is greater than he who does.' Therefore, the *Schnorrer* who causes charity is even greater than he who gives it."

"Talk of de devil," said Yankelé, who had much difficulty in keeping his countenance when Manasseh became magnificent and dithyrambic. "Vy, dere is Greenbaum, whose fader vas buried yesterday. Let us cross over by accident and vish him long life."

"Greenbaum dead! Was that the Greenbaum on 'Change, who was such a rascal with the wenches?"

"De same," said Yankelé. Then approaching the son, he cried, "Good Sabbath, Mr. Greenbaum; I vish you long life. Vat a blow for de community!"

"It comforts me to hear you say so," said the son, with a sob in his voice.

"Ah, yes!" said Yankelé chokingly. "Your fader vas a great and good man — just my size."

"I've already given them away to Baruch the glazier," replied the mourner.

"But he has his glaziering," remonstrated Yankelé. "I have noting but de clothes I stand in, and dey don't fit me half so vell as your fader's vould have done."

"Baruch has been very unfortunate," replied Greenbaum defensively. "He had a misfortune in the winter, and he has never got straight yet. A child of his died, and, unhappily, just when the snowballing was at its height, so that he lost seven days by the mourning." And he moved away.

"Did I not say work was uncertain?" cried Manasseh.

"Not all," maintained the *Schnorrer*. "What of de six guineas I make by carrying round de Palm-branch on Tabernacles to be shaken by de voomans who cannot attend Synagogue, and by blowing de trumpet for de same voomans on New Year, so dat dey may break deir fasts?"

"The amount is too small to deserve discussion. Pass on."

"Dere is a smaller amount — just half dat — I get from de presents to de poor at de Feast of Lots, and from de Bridegrooms of de Beginning and de Bridegrooms of de Law at de Rejoicing of de Law, and dere is about four pounds ten a year from de sale of clothes given to me. Den I have a lot o' meals given me — dis, I have reckoned, is as good as seven pounds. And, lastly, I cannot count de odds and ends under ten guineas. You know dere are alvays legacies, gifts, distributions — all unexpected. You never know who'll break out next."

"Yes, I think it's not too high a percentage of your income to expect from unexpected sources," admitted Manasseh. "I have myself lingered about 'Change Alley or Sampson's Coffee House just when the jobbers have pulled off a special coup, and they have paid me quite a high percentage on their profits."

"And I," boasted Yankelé, stung to noble emulation, "have made two sov'rans in von minute out of Gideon de bullion-broker. He likes to give *Schnorrers* sov'rans, as if in mistake for shillings, to see vat dey'll do. De fools hurry off, or move slowly avay, as if not noticing, or put it quickly in de pocket. But dose who have visdom tell him he's made a mistake, and he gives dem anoder sov'ran. Honesty is de best policy with Gideon. Den dere is Rabbi de Falk, de Baal Shem — de great Cabbalist. Ven — "

"But," interrupted Manasseh impatiently, "you haven't made out your hundred and fifty a year."

Yankelé's face fell. "Not if you cut out so many items."

"No, but even all inclusive it only comes to a hundred and forty-three pounds nineteen shillings."

"Nonsense!" said Yankelé, staggered. "How can you know so exact?"

"Do you think I cannot do simple addition?" responded Manasseh sternly. "Are not these your ten items?"

		£	s.	d.
1.	Synagogue Pension, with Passover extras	8	0	0
2.	Synagogue-knocking	10	10	0
3.	District Visiting	65	0	0
4.	As Congregation-man and Pyx-bearer	14	0	0
5.	Year-Times	15	0	0
6.	Palm-branch and Trumpet Fees	6	6	0
7.	Purim-presents, &c.	3	3	0
8.	Sale of Clothes	4	10	0
9.	Equivalent of Free Meals	7	0	0
10.	Miscellanea, the unexpected	10	10	0
	Total	£143	19	0

"A child could sum it up," concluded Manasseh severely. Yankelé was subdued to genuine respect and consternation by da Costa's marvellous memory and arithmetical genius. But he rallied immediately. "Of course, I also reckoned on a dowry mid my bride, if only a hundred pounds."

"Well, invested in Consols, that would not bring you four pounds more," replied Manasseh instantly.

"The rest vill be made up in extra free meals," Yankelé answered no less quickly. "For ven I take your daughter off your hands you vill be able to afford to invite me more often to your table dan you do now."

"Not at all," retorted Manasseh, "for now that I know how well off you are I shall no longer feel I am doing a charity."

"Oh, yes, you vill," said Yankelé insinuatingly. "You are too much a man of honour to know as a private philantropist vat I have told de marriage-broker, de fader-in-law and de fellow *Schnorrer*. Besides, I vould have de free meals from you as de son-in-law, not de *Schnorrer*."

"In that relation I should also have free meals from you," rejoined Manasseh.

"I never dared to tink you vould do me de honour. But even so I can never give you such good meals as you give me. So dere is still a balance in my favour."

"That is true," said da Costa thoughtfully. "But you have still about a guinea to make up."

Yankelé was driven into a corner at last. But he flashed back, without perceptible pause, "You do not allow for vat I save by my piety. I fast twenty times a year, and surely dat is at least anoder guinea per annum."

"But you will have children," retorted da Costa.

Yankelé shrugged his shoulders.

"Dat is de affair of de Holy One, blessed be He. Ven He sends dem He vill provide for dem. You must not forget, too, dat mid *your* daughter de dowry vould be noting so small as a hundred pounds."

"My daughter will have a dowry befitting her station, certainly," said Manasseh, with his grandest manner; "but then I had looked forward to her marrying a king of *Schnorrers*."

"Vell, but ven I marry her I shall be."

"How so?"

"I shall have *schnorred* your daughter — the most precious thing in the world! And *schnorred* her from a king of *Schnorrers*, too!! And I shall have *schnorred* your services as marriage-broker into de bargain ! ! ! "

CHAPTER IV

SHOWING HOW THE ROYAL WEDDING WAS ARRANGED

MANASSEH BUENO BARZILLAI AZEVEDO DA COSTA was so impressed by his would-be son-in-law's last argument that he perpended it in silence for a full minute. When he replied, his tone showed even more respect than had been infused into it by the statement of the aspirant's income. Manasseh was not of those to whom money is a fetish; he regarded it merely as something to be had for the asking. It was intellect for which he reserved his admiration. That was strictly not transferable.

"It is true," he said, "that if I yielded to your importunities and gave you my daughter, you would thereby have approved yourself a king of *Schnorrers,* of a rank suitable to my daughter's, but an analysis of your argument will show that you are begging the question."

"Vat more proof do you vant of my begging powers?" demanded Yankelé, spreading out his palms and shrugging his shoulders.

"Much greater proof," replied Manasseh. "I ought to have some instance of your powers. The only time I have seen you try to *schnorr* you failed."

"Me! ven?" exclaimed Yankelé indignantly.

"Why, this very night. When you asked young Greenbaum for his dead father's clothes!"

"But he had already given them away!" protested the Pole.

"What of that? If anyone had given away *my* clothes, I should have demanded compensation. You must really be above rebuffs of that kind, Yankelé, if you are to be my son-in-law. No, no, I

51

remember the dictum of the Sages: 'To give your daughter to an uncultured man is like throwing her bound to a lion.' ''

"But you have also seen me *schnorr* mid success," remonstrated the suitor.

"Never!" protested Manasseh vehemently.

"Often!"

"From whom?"

"From you!" said Yankelé boldly.

"From *me!*" sneered Manasseh, accentuating the pronoun with infinite contempt. "What does that prove? I am a generous man. The test is to *schnorr* from a miser."

"I *vill schnorr* from a miser!" announced Yankelé desperately.

"You will!"

"Yes. Choose your miser."

"No, I leave it to you," said da Costa politely.

"Vell, Sam Lazarus, de butcher shop!"

"No, not Sam Lazarus, he once gave a *Schnorrer* I know elevenpence."

"Elevenpence?" incredulously murmured Yankelé.

"Yes, it was the only way he could pass a shilling. It wasn't bad, only cracked, but he could get no one to take it except a *Schnorrer.* He made the man give him a penny change though. 'Tis true the man afterwards laid out the shilling at Lazarus's shop. Still a really great miser would have added that cracked shilling to his hoard rather than the perfect penny."

"No," argued Yankelé, "dere vould be no difference, since he does not spend."

"True," said da Costa reflectively, "but by that same token a miser is not the most difficult person to tackle."

"How do you make dat out?"

"Is it not obvious? Already we see Lazarus giving away elevenpence. A miser who spends nothing on himself may, in exceptional cases, be induced to give away something. It is the man who indulges himself in every luxury and gives away nothing who is the hardest to *schnorr* from. He has a *use* for his money — himself! If you diminish his store you hurt him in the tenderest part — you rob him of creature comforts. To *schnorr* from such a one I should regard as a higher and nobler thing than to *schnorr* from a mere miser."

"Vell, name your man."

"No — I couldn't think of taking it out of your hands," said Manasseh again with his stately bow. "Whomever you select I will abide by. If I could not rely on your honour, would I dream of you as a son-in-law?"

"Den I vill go to Mendel Jacobs, of Mary Axe."

"Mendel Jacobs — oh, no! Why, he's married! A married man cannot be entirely devoted to himself."

"Vy not? Is not a vife a creature comfort? P'raps also she comes cheaper dan a housekeeper."

"We will not argue it. I will not have Mendel Jacobs."

"Simon Kelutski, de vine-merchant."

"He! He is quite generous with his snuff-box. I have myself been offered a pinch. Of course I did not accept it."

Yankéle selected several other names, but Manasseh barred them all, and at last had an inspiration of his own.

"Isn't there a Rabbi in your community whose stinginess is proverbial? Let me see, what's his name?"

"A Rabbi!" murmured Yankéle disingenuously, while his heart began to palpitate with alarm.

"Yes, isn't there — Rabbi Bloater!"

Yankelé shook his head. Ruin stared him in the face — his fondest hopes were crumbling.

"I know it's some fishy name—Rabbi Haddock—no it isn't. It's Rabbi Remorse something."

Yankelé saw it was all over with him.

"P'raps you mean Rabbi Remorse Red-herring," he said feebly, for his voice failed him.

"Ah, yes! Rabbi Remorse Red-herring," said Manasseh. "From all I hear — for I have never seen the man — a king of guzzlers and topers, and the meanest of mankind. Now if you could dine with *him* you might indeed be called a king of *Schnorrers*."

Yankelé was pale and trembling. "But *he* is married!" he urged, with a happy thought.

"Dine with him to-morrow'," said Manasseh inexorably. "He fares extra royally on the Sabbath. Obtain admission to his table, and you shall be admitted into my family."

"But you do not know the man — it is impossible!" cried Yankelé.

"That is the excuse of the bad *Schnorrer*. You have heard my ultimatum. No dinner, no wife. No wife—no dowry!"

"Vat vould dis dowry be?" asked Yankelé, by way of diversion.

"Oh, unique — quite unique. First of all there would be all the money she gets from the Synagogue. Our Synagogue gives considerable dowries to portionless girls. There are large bequests for the purpose."

Yankelé's eyes glittered.

"Ah, vat gentlemen you Spaniards be!"

"Then I daresay I should hand over to my son-in-law all my Jerusalem land."

"Have you property in de Holy Land?" said Yankelé.

"First class, with an unquestionable title. And, of course, I would give you some province or other in this country."

"What!" gasped Yankelé.

"Could I do less?" said Manasseh blandly. "My own flesh and blood, remember! Ah, here is my door. It is too late to ask you in. Good Sabbath! Don't forget your appointment to dine with Rabbi Remorse Red-herring tomorrow."

"Good Sabbath!" faltered Yankelé, and crawled home heavy-hearted to Dinah's Buildings, Tripe Yard, Whitechapel, where the memory of him lingers even unto this day.

Rabbi Remorse Red-herring was an unofficial preacher who officiated at mourning services in private houses, having a gift of well-turned eulogy. He was a big, burly man with overlapping stomach and a red beard, and his spiritual consolations drew tears. His client knew him to be vastly self-indulgent in private life, and abstemious in the matter of benevolence; but they did not confound the *rôles*. As a mourning preacher he gave every satisfaction: he was regular and punctual, and did not keep the congregation waiting, and he had had considerable experience in showing that there was yet balm in Gilead.

He had about five ways of showing it — the variants depending upon the circumstances. If, as not infrequently happened, the person deceased was a stranger to him, he would enquire in the passage: "Was it man or woman? Boy or girl? Married or single? Any children? Young 'uns or old 'uns?"

When these questions had been answered, he was ready. He knew exactly which of his five consolatory addresses to deliver — they were all sufficiently vague and general to cover considerable variety of circumstance, and even when he misheard the replies in the passage, and dilated on the grief of a departed widower's relict, the results were not fatal throughout. The few impossible passages might be explained by the mishearing of the audience. Sometimes — very rarely — he would venture on a supplementary sentence or two fitting the specific occasion, but very cautiously, for a man with a reputation for extempore addresses cannot be too wary of speaking on the spur of the moment.

Off obituary lines he was a failure; at any rate, his one attempt to preach from an English Synagogue pulpit resulted in a nickname. His theme was Remorse, which he explained with much care to the congregation.

"For instance," said the preacher, "the other day I was walking over London Bridge, when I saw a fishwife standing with a basket of red-herrings. I says, 'How much?' She says, 'Two for three-halfpence.' I says, 'Oh, that's frightfully dear! I can easily get three for twopence.' But she wouldn't part with them at that price, so I went on, thinking I'd meet another woman with a similar lot over the water. They were lovely fat herrings, and my chaps watered in anticipation of the treat of eating them. But when I got to the other end of the bridge there was no other fishwife to be seen. So I resolved to turn back to the first fishwife, for, after all, I reflected, the herrings were really very cheap, and I had only complained in the way of business. But when I got back the woman was just sold out. I could have torn my hair with vexation. Now, that's what I called Remorse."

After that the Rabbi was what the congregation called Remorse; also Red-herring.

The Rabbi's fondness for concrete exemplification of abstract ideas was not, however, to be stifled, and there was one illustration of Charity which found a place in all the five sermons of consolation.

"If you have a pair of old breeches, send them to the Rabbi."

Rabbi Remorse Red-herring was, however, as is the way of preachers, himself aught but a concrete exemplification of the virtues he inculcated. He lived generously — through other people's generosity — but no one could boast of having received a farthing from him over and above what was due to them; while *Schnorrers* (who deemed considerable sums due to them) regarded him in the light of.a defalcating bankrupt. He, for his part, had a countervailing grudge against the world, fancying the work he did for it but feebly remunerated. "I get so little," ran his bitter plaint, "that I couldn't live, *if it were not for the fasts.*" And, indeed, the fasts of the religion were worth much more to him than to Yankelé; his meals were so profuse that his savings from this source were quite a little revenue. As Yankelé had pointed out, he was married. And his wife had given him a child, but it died at the age of seven, bequeathing to him the only poignant sorrow of his life. He was too jealous to call in a rival consolation preacher during those dark days, and none of his own five sermons seemed to fit the case. It was some months before he took his meals regularly.

At no time had anyone else taken meals in his house, except by law entitled. Though she had only two to cook for, his wife habitually provided for three, counting her husband no mere unit. Herself she reckoned as a half.

It was with intelligible perturbation, therefore, that Yankelé, dressed in some other man's best, approached the house of Rabbi Remorse Red-herring about a quarter of an hour before the Sabbath mid-day meal, intent on sharing it with him.

"No dinner, no marriage!" was da Costa's stern ukase.

What wonder if the inaccessible meal took upon itself the grandiosity of a wedding feast! Deborah da Costa's lovely face tantalised him like a mirage.

The Sabbath day was bleak, but chiller was his heart. The Rabbi had apartments in Steward Street, Spitalfields, an elegant suite on the ground-floor, for he stinted himself in nothing but charity. At the entrance was a porch — a pointed Gothic arch of wood supported by two pillars. As Yankelé mounted the three wooden steps, breathing as painfully as if they were three hundred, and wondering if he would ever get merely as far as the other side of the door, he was assailed by the temptation to go and dine peacefully at home, and represent to da Costa that he had feasted with the Rabbi. Manasseh would never know, Manasseh had taken no steps to ascertain if he satisfied the test or not. Such carelessness, he told himself in righteous indignation, deserved fitting punishment. But, on the other hand, he recalled Manasseh's trust in him; Manasseh believed him a man of honour, and the patron's elevation of soul awoke an answering chivalry in the parasite.

He decided to make the attempt at least, for there would be plenty of time to say he had succeeded, after he had failed.

Vibrating with tremors of nobility as well as of apprehension, Yankelé lifted the knocker. He had no programme, trusting to chance and mother-wit.

Mrs. Remorse Red-herring half opened the door.

"I vish to see de Rabbi," he said, putting one foot within.

"He is engaged," said the wife — a tiny thin creature who had been plump and pretty. "He is very busy talking with a gentleman."

"Oh, but I can vait."

"But the Rabbi will be having his dinner soon."

"I can vait till after dinner," said Yankelé obligingly.

"Oh, but the Rabbi sits long at table."

"I don't mind," said Yankelé with undiminished placidity, "de longer de better."

The poor woman looked perplexed. "I'll tell my husband," she said at last.

Yankelé had an anxious moment in the passage.

"The Rabbi wishes to know what you want," she said when she returned.

"I vant to get married," said Yankelé with an inspiration of veracity.

"But my husband doesn't marry people."

"Vy not?"

"He only brings consolations into households," she explained ingenuously.

"Vell, I won't get married midout him," Yankelé murmured lugubriously.

The little woman went back in bewilderment to her bosom's lord. Forthwith out came Rabbi Remorse Red-herring, curiosity and cupidity in his eyes. He wore the skullcap of sanctity, but looked the gourmand in spite of it.

"Good Sabbath, sir! What is this about your getting married?"

"It's a long story," said Yankelé, "and as your good vife told me your dinner is just ready, I mustn't keep you now."

"No, there are still a few minutes before dinner. What is it?"

Yankelé shook his head. "I couldn't tink of keeping you in dis draughty passage."

"I don't mind. I don't feel any draught."

"Dat's just vere de danger lays. You don't notice, and one day you find yourself laid up mid rheumatism, and you vill have

Remorse," said Yankelé with a twinkle. "Your life is precious —
if *you* die, who vill console de community?"

It was an ambiguous remark, but the Rabbi understood it in
its most flattering sense, and his little eyes beamed. "I would ask
you inside," he said, "but I have a visitor."

"No matter," said Yankelé, "vat I have to say to you, Rabbi,
is not private. A stranger may hear it."

Still undecided, the Rabbi muttered, "You want me to marry
you?"

"I have come to get married," replied Yankelé.

"But I have never been called upon to marry people."

"It's never too late to mend, dey say."

"Strange — strange," murmured the Rabbi reflectively.

"Vat is strange?"

"That you should come to me just to-day. But why did you
not go to Rabbi Sandman?"

"Rabbi Sandman!" replied Yankelé with contempt. "Vere
vould be de good of going to him?"

"But why not?"

"Every *Schnorrer* goes to him," said Yankelé frankly.

"Hum!" mused the Rabbi. "Perhaps there *is* an opening for a
more select marrier. Come in, then, I can give you five minutes
if you really don't mind talking before a stranger."

He threw open the door, and led the way into the sitting-
room.

Yankelé followed, exultant; the outworks were already carried,
and his heart beat high with hope. But at his first glance within,
he reeled and almost fell.

Standing with his back to the fire and dominating the room
was Manasseh Bueno Barzillai Azevedo da Costa!

"Ah, Yankelé, good Sabbath!" said da Costa affably.

"G-g-ood Sabbath!" stammered Yankelé.

"Why, you know each other!" cried the Rabbi.

"Oh, yes," said Manasseh, "an acquaintance of yours, too,
apparently."

"No, he is just come to see me about something," replied the
Rabbi.

"I thought you did not know the Rabbi, Mr. da Costa?"
Yankelé could not help saying.

"I didn't. I only had the pleasure of making his acquaintance half an hour ago. I met him in the street as he was coming home from morning service, and he was kind enough to invite me to dinner."

Yankelé gasped; despite his secret amusement at Manasseh's airs, there were moments when the easy magnificence of the man overwhelmed him, extorted his reluctant admiration. How in Heaven's name had the Spaniard conquered at a blow!

Looking down at the table, he now observed that it was already laid for dinner — and for three! He should have been that third. Was it fair of Manasseh to handicap him thus? Naturally, there would be infinitely less chance of a fourth being invited than a third — to say nothing of the dearth of provisions. "But, surely, you don't intend to stay to dinner!" he complained in dismay.

"I have given my word," said Manasseh, "and I shouldn't care to disappoint the Rabbi."

"Oh, it's no disappointment, no disappointment," remarked Rabbi Remorse Red-herring cordially, "I could just as well come round and see you after dinner."

"After dinner I never see people," said Manasseh majestically; "I sleep."

The Rabbi dared not make further protest: he turned to Yankelé and asked, "Well, now, what's this about your marriage?"

"I can't tell you before Mr. da Costa," replied Yankelé, to gain time.

"Why not? You said anybody might hear."

"Noting of the sort. I said a stranger might hear. But Mr. da Costa isn't a stranger. He knows too much about de matter."

"What shall we do, then?" murmured the Rabbi.

"I can vait till after dinner," said Yankelé, with good-natured carelessness. "*I* don't sleep—"

Before the Rabbi could reply, the wife brought in a baked dish, and set it on the table. Her husband glowered at her, but she, regular as clockwork, and as unthinking, produced the black bottle of *schnapps*. It was her husband's business to get rid of Yankelé; her business was to bring on the dinner. If she had delayed, he would have raged equally. She was not only wife, but maid-of-all-work.

Seeing the advanced state of the preparations, Manasseh da

Costa took his seat at the table; obeying her husband's signifi-
cant glance, Mrs. Red-herring took up her position at the foot.
The Rabbi himself sat down at the head, behind the dish. He
always served, being the only person he could rely upon to gauge
his capacities. Yankelé was left standing. The odour of the meat
and potatoes impregnated the atmosphere with wistful poetry.

Suddenly the Rabbi looked up and perceived Yankelé. "Will
you do as we do?" he said in seductive accents.

The *Schnorrer's* heart gave one wild, mad throb of joy. He
laid his hand on the only other chair.

"I don't mind if I do," he said, with responsive amiability.

"Then go home and have *your* dinner," said the Rabbi.

Yankelé's wild heart-beat was exchanged for a stagnation as of
death. A shiver ran down his spine. He darted an agonised ap-
pealing glance at Manasseh, who sniggered inscrutably.

"Oh, I don't tink I ought to go avay and leave you midout a
tird man for grace," he said, in tones of prophetic rebuke. "Since
I *be* here, it vould be a sin not to stay."

The Rabbi, having a certain connection with religion, was
cornered; he was not able to repudiate such an opportunity of
that more pious form of grace which needs the presence of three
males.

"Oh, I should be very glad for you to stay," said the Rabbi,
but, unfortunately, we have only three meat-plates."

"Oh, de dish vill do for me."

"Very well, then!" said the Rabbi.

And Yankelé, with the old mad heart-beat, took the fourth
chair, darting a triumphant glance at the still sniggering Manasseh.

The hostess rose, misunderstanding her husband's optical sig-
nals, and fished out a knife and fork from the recesses of a chif-
fonier. The host first heaped his own plate high with artistically
coloured potatoes and stiff meat — less from discourtesy than
from life-long habit — then divided the remainder in unequal
portions between Manasseh and the little woman, in rough cor-
respondence with their sizes. Finally, he handed Yankelé the
empty dish.

"You see there is nothing left," he said simply. "We didn't
even expect one visitor."

"First come, first served," observed Manasseh, with his sphinx-like expression, as he fell-to.

Yankelé sat frozen, staring blankly at the dish, his brain as empty. He had lost.

Such a dinner was a hollow mockery — like the dish. He could not expect Manasseh to accept it, quibbled he ever so cunningly. He sat for a minute or two as in a dream, the music of knife and fork ringing mockingly in his ears, his hungry palate moistened by the delicious savour. Then he shook off his stupor, and all his being was desperately astrain, questing for an idea. Manasseh discoursed with his host on neo-Hebrew literature.

"We thought of starting a journal at Grodno," said the Rabbi, "only the funds — "

"Be you den a native of Grodno?" interrupted Yankelé.

"Yes, I was born there," mumbled the Rabbi, "but I left there twenty years ago." His mouth was full, and he did not cease to ply the cutlery.

"Ah!" said Yankelé enthusiastically, "den you must be de famous preacher everybody speaks of. I do not remember you myself, for I vas a boy, but dey say ve haven't got no such preachers nowaday."

"In Grodno my husband kept a brandy shop," put in the hostess.

There was a bad quarter of a minute of silence. To Yankelé's relief, the Rabbi ended it by observing, "Yes, but doubtless the gentleman (you will excuse me calling you that, sir, I don't know your real name) alluded to my fame as a boy-Maggid. At the age of five I preached to audiences of many hundreds, and my manipulation of texts, my demonstrations that they did not mean what they said, drew tears even from octogenarians familiar with the Torah from their earliest infancy. It was said there never was such a wonder-child since Ben Sira."

"But why did you give it up?" enquired Manasseh.

"It gave me up," said the Rabbi, putting down his knife and fork to expound an ancient grievance. "A boy-Maggid cannot last more than a few years. Up to nine I was still a draw, but every year the wonder grew less, and, when I was thirteen, my Bar-Mitzvah (confirmation) sermon occasioned no more sensation than those of the many other lads whose sermons I had written for them. I struggled along as boyishly as I could for some time after that, but it was in a losing cause. My age won on me daily. As it is said, 'I have been young, and now I am old.' In vain I composed the most eloquent addresses to be heard in Grodno. In vain I gave a course on the emotions, with explanations and instances from daily life — the fickle public preferred younger attractions. So at last I gave it up and sold *vodki.*"

"Vat a pity! Vat a pity!" ejaculated Yankelé, "after vinning fame in de Torah!"

"But what is a man to do? He is not always a boy," replied the Rabbi. "Yes, I kept a brandy shop. That's what I call Degradation. But there is always balm in Gilead. I lost so much money over it that I had to emigrate to England, where, finding nothing else to do, I became a preacher again." He poured himself out a glass of *schnapps,* ignoring the water.

"I heard nothing of de *vodki* shop," said Yankelé; "it vas svallowed up in your earlier fame."

The Rabbi drained the glass of *schnapps,* smacked his lips, and resumed his knife and fork. Manasseh reached for the unoffered bottle, and helped himself liberally. The Rabbi unostentatiously withdrew it beyond his easy reach, looking at Yankelé the while.

"How long have you been in England?" he asked the Pole.

"Not long," said Yankelé.

"Ha! Does Gabriel the cantor still suffer fom neuralgia?"

Yankelé looked sad. "No — he is dead," he said.

"Dear me! Well, he was tottering when I knew him. His blowing of the ram's horn got wheezier every year. And how is his young brother, Samuel?"

"He is dead!" said Yankelé.

"What, he too! Tut, tut! He was so robust. Has Mendelssohn, the stonemason, got many more girls?"

"He is dead!" said Yankelé.

"Nonsense!" gasped the Rabbi, dropping his knife and fork. "Why, I heard from him only a few months ago."

"He is dead!" said Yankelé.

"Good gracious me! Mendelssohn dead!" After a moment of emotion he resumed his meal. "But his sons and daughters are all doing well, I hope. The eldest, Solomon, was a most pious youth, and his third girl, Neshamah, promised to be a rare beauty."

"They are dead!" said Yankelé.

This time the Rabbi turned pale as a corpse himself. He laid down his knife and fork automatically.

"D — dead," he breathed in an awestruck whisper. "All?"

"Everyone. De same cholera took all de family."

The Rabbi covered his face with his hands. "Then poor Solomon's wife is a widow. I hope he left her enough to live upon."

"No, but it doesn't matter," said Yankelé.

"It matters a great deal," cried the Rabbi.

"She is dead," said Yankelé.

"Rebecca Schwartz dead!" screamed the Rabbi, for he had once loved the maiden himself, and, not having married her, had still a tenderness for her.

"Rebecca Schwartz," repeated Yankelé inexorably.

"Was it the cholera?" faltered the Rabbi.

"No, she vas heartbroke."

Rabbi Remorse Red-herring silently pushed his plate away, and leaned his elbows upon the table and his face upon his palms, and his chin upon the bottle of *schnapps* in mournful meditation.

"You are not eating, Rabbi," said Yankelé insinuatingly.

"I have lost my appetite," said the Rabbi.

"Vat a pity to let food get cold and spoil! You'd better eat it."

The Rabbi shook his head querulously.

"Den I vill eat it," cried Yankelé indignantly. "Good hot food like dat!"

"As you like," said the Rabbi wearily. And Yankelé began to eat at lightning speed, pausing only to wink at the inscrutable Manasseh; and to cast yearning glances at the inaccessible *schnapps* that supported the Rabbi's chin.

Presently the Rabbi looked up: "You're quite sure all these people are dead?" he asked with a dawning suspicion.

"May my blood be poured out like this *schnapps*," protested Yankelé, dislodging the bottle, and vehemently pouring the spirit into a tumbler, "if dey be not."

The Rabbi relapsed into his moody attitude, and retained it till his wife brought in a big willow-pattern china dish of stewed prunes and pippins. She produced four plates for these, and so

Yankelé finished his meal in the unquestionable status of a first-class guest. The Rabbi was by this time sufficiently recovered to toy with two platefuls in a melancholy silence which he did not break till his mouth opened involuntarily to intone the grace.

When grace was over he turned to Manasseh and said, "And what was this way you were suggesting to me of getting a profitable Sephardic connection?"

"I did, indeed, wonder why you did not extend your practice as consolation preacher among the Spanish Jews," replied Manasseh gravely. "But after what we have just heard of the death-rate of Jews in Grodno, I should seriously advise you to go back there."

"No, they cannot forget that I was once a boy," replied the Rabbi with equal gravity. "I prefer the Spanish Jews. They are all well-to-do. They may not die so often as the Russians, but they die better, so to speak. You will give me introductions, you will speak of me to your illustrious friends, I understand."

"You understand!" repeated Manasseh in dignified astonishment. "You do not understand. I shall do no such thing."

"But you yourself suggested it!" cried the Rabbi excitedly.

"I? Nothing of the kind. I had heard of you and your ministrations to mourners, and meeting you in the street this afternoon for the first time, it struck me to enquire why you did not carry your consolations into the bosom of my community where so much more money is to be made. I said I wondered you had not done so from the first. And you — invited me to dinner. I still wonder. That is all, my good man." He rose to go.

The haughty rebuke silenced the Rabbi, though his heart was hot with a vague sense of injury.

"Do you come my way, Yankelé?" said Manasseh carelessly.

The Rabbi turned hastily to his second guest.

"When do you want me to marry you?" he asked.

"You have married me," replied Yankelé.

"I?" gasped the Rabbi. It was the last straw.

"Yes," reiterated Yankelé. "Hasn't he, Mr. da Costa?" His heart went pit-a-pat as he put the question.

"Certainly," said Manasseh without hesitation.

Yankelé's face was made glorious summer. Only two of the quartette knew the secret of his radiance.

"There, Rabbi," he cried exultantly. "Good Sabbath!"

"Good Sabbath!" added Manasseh.

"Good Sabbath," dazedly murmured the Rabbi.

"Good Sabbath," added his wife.

"Congratulate me!" cried Yankelé when they got outside.

"On what?" asked Manasseh.

"On being your future son-in-law, of course."

"Oh, on *that?* Certainly, I congratulate you most heartily." The two *Schnorrers* shook hands. "I thought you were asking for compliments on your manœuvering."

"Vy, doesn't it deserve dem?"

"No," said Manasseh magisterially.

"No?" queried Yankelé, his heart sinking again. "Vy not?"

"Why did you kill so many people?"

"Somebody must die dat I may live."

"You said that before," said Manasseh severely. "A good *Schnorrer* would not have slaughtered so many for his dinner. It is a waste of good material. And then you told lies!"

"How do you know they are not dead?" pleaded Yankelé.

The King shook his head reprovingly. "A first-class *Schnorrer* never lies," he laid it down.

"I might have made truth go as far as a lie — if you hadn't come to dinner yourself."

"What is that you say? Why, I came to encourage you by showing you how easy your task was."

"On de contrary, you made it much harder for me. Dere vas no dinner left."

"But against that you must reckon that since the Rabbi had already invited one person, he couldn't be so hard to tackle as I had fancied."

"Oh, but you must not judge from yourself," protested Yankelé. "You be not a *Schnorrer* — you be a miracle."

"But I should like a miracle for my son-in-law also," grumbled the King.

"And if you had to *schnorr* a son-in-law, you vould get a miracle," said Yankelé soothingly. "As he has to *schnorr* you, *he* gets the miracle."

"True," observed Manasseh musingly, "and I think you might therefore be very well content without the dowry."

"So I might," admitted Yankelé, "only *you* vould not be content to break your promise. I suppose I shall have some of de dowry on de marriage morning."

"On that morning you shall get my daughter — without fail. Surely that will be enough for one day!"

"Vell, ven do I get de money your daughter gets from de Synagogue?"

"When she gets it from the Synagogue, of course."

"How much vill it be?"

"It may be a hundred and fifty pounds," said Manasseh pompously.

Yankelé's eyes sparkled.

"And it may be less," added Manasseh as an after-thought.

"How much less?" enquired Yankelé anxiously.

"A hundred and fifty pounds," repeated Manasseh pompously.

"D'you mean to say I may get noting?"

"Certainly, if she gets nothing. What I promised you was the money she gets from the Synagogue. Should she be fortunate enough in the *sorteo* — "

"De *sorteo*! Vat is dat?"

"The dowry I told you of. It is accorded by lot. My daughter has as good a chance as any other maiden. By winning her you stand to win a hundred and fifty pounds. It is a handsome amount. There are not many fathers who would do as much for their daughters," concluded Manasseh with conscious magnanimity.

"But about de Jerusalem estate!" said Yankelé, shifting his standpoint. "I don't vant to go and live dere. De Messiah is not yet come."

"No, you will hardly be able to live on it," admitted Manasseh.

"You do not object to my selling it, den?"

"Oh, no! If you are so sordid, if you have no true Jewish sentiment!"

"Ven can I come into possession?"

"On the wedding day if you like."

"One may as vell get it over," said Yankelé, suppressing a desire to rub his hands in glee. "As de Talmud says, 'One peppercorn to-day is better dan a basketful of pumpkins to-morrow.' "

"All right! I will bring it to the Synagogue."

"Bring it to de Synagogue!" repeated Yankelé in amaze. "Oh, you mean de deed of transfer."

"The deed of transfer! Do you think I waste my substance on solicitors? No, I will bring the property itself."

"But how can you do dat?"

"Where is the difficulty?" demanded Manasseh with withering contempt. "Surely a child could carry a casket of Jerusalem earth to Synagogue!"

"A casket of earth! Is your property in Jerusalem only a casket of earth?"

"What then? You didn't expect it would be a casket of diamonds?" retorted Manasseh, with gathering wrath. "To a true Jew a casket of Jerusalem earth is worth all the diamonds in the world."

"But your Jerusalem property is a fraud!" gasped Yankelé.

"Oh, no, you may be easy on that point. It's quite genuine. I know there is a good deal of spurious Palestine earth in circulation, and that many a dead man who has clods of it thrown into his tomb is nevertheless buried in unholy soil. But this casket I was careful to obtain from a Rabbi of extreme sanctity. It was the only thing he had worth *schnorring*."

"I don't suppose I shall get more dan a crown for it," said Yankelé, with irrepressible indignation.

"That's what I say," returned Manasseh; "and never did I think a son-in-law of mine would meditate selling my holy soil for a paltry five shillings! I will not withdraw my promise, but I am disappointed in you — bitterly disappointed. Had I known this earth was not to cover your bones, it should have gone down to the grave with me, as enjoined in my last will and testament, by the side of which it stands in my safe."

"Very vell, I von't sell it," said Yankelé sulkily.

"You relieve my soul. As the *Mishnah* says, 'He who marries a wife for money begets froward children.' "

"And vat about de province in England?" asked Yankelé, in low, despondent tones. He had never believed in *that,* but now, behind all his despair and incredulity, was a vague hope that something might yet be saved from the crash.

"Oh, you shall choose your own," replied Manasseh graciously. "We will get a large map of London, and I will mark off in red pencil the domain in which I *schnorr*. You will then choose any district in this — say, two main streets and a dozen byways and alleys — which shall be marked off in blue pencil, and whatever province of my kingdom you pick, I undertake not to *schnorr* in, from your wedding-day onwards. I need not tell you how valuable such a province already is; under careful administration, such as you would be able to give it, the revenue from it might be doubled, trebled. I do not think your tribute to me need be more than ten per cent."

Yankelé walked along mesmerised, reduced to somnambulism by his magnificently masterful patron.

"Oh, here we are!" said Manasseh, stopping short. "Won't you come in and see the bride, and wish her joy?"

A flash of joy came into Yankelé's own face, dissipating his glooms. After all there was always da Costa's beautiful daughter — a solid, substantial satisfaction. He was glad she was not an item of the dowry.

The unconscious bride opened the door.

"Ah, ha, Yankelé!" said Manasseh, his paternal heart aglow at the sight of her loveliness. "You will be not only a king, but a rich king. As it is written, 'Who is rich? He who hath a beautiful wife.' "

CHAPTER V

MANASSEH DA COSTA (thus docked of his nominal plenitude in the solemn writ) had been summoned before the Mahamad, the intended union of his daughter with a Polish Jew having excited the liveliest horror and displeasure in the breasts of the Elders of the Synagogue. Such a Jew did not pronounce Hebrew as they did!

The Mahamad was a Council of Five, no less dread than the more notorious Council of Ten. Like the Venetian Tribunal, which has unjustly monopolised the attention of history, it was of annual election, and it was elected by a larger body of Elders, just as the Council of Ten was chosen by the aristocracy. "The gentlemen of the Mahamad," as they were styled, administered the affairs of the Spanish-Portuguese community, and their oligarchy would undoubtedly be a byword for all that is arbitrary and inquisitorial but for the widespread ignorance of its existence. To itself the Mahamad was the centre of creation. On one occasion it refused to bow even to the authority of the Lord Mayor of London. A Sephardic Jew lived and moved and had his being "by permission of the Mahamad." Without its consent he could have no legitimate place in the scheme of things. Minus "the permission of the Mahamad" he could not marry; with it he could be divorced readily. He might, indeed, die without the sanction of the Council of Five, but this was the only great act of his life which was free from its surveillance, and he could certainly not be buried save "by permission of the Mahamad." The Haham himself, the Sage or Chief Rabbi of the con-

gregation, could not unite his flock in holy wedlock without the
"permission of the Mahamad." And this authority was not
merely negative and passive, it was likewise positive and active.
To be a Yahid — a recognised congregant — one had to submit
one's neck to a yoke more galling even than that of the Torah,
to say nothing of the payment of Finta, or poll-tax. Woe to him
who refused to be Warden of the Captives — he who ransomed
the chained hostages of the Moorish Corsairs, or the war prison-
ers held in durance by the Turks — or to be President of the
Congregation, or Parnass of the Holy Land, or Bridegroom of
the Law, or any of the numerous dignitaries of a complex constitution. Fines, frequent and heavy — for the benefit of the
poor-box — awaited him "by permission of the Mahamad." Unhappy the wight who misconducted himself in Synagogue "by
offending the president, or grossly insulting any other person,"
as the ordinance deliciously ran. Penalties, stringent and harry-
ing, visited these and other offences — deprivation of the "good
deeds," of swathing the Holy Scroll, or opening the Ark; igno-
minious relegation to seats behind the reading-desk, withdrawal of
the franchise, prohibition against shaving for a term of weeks!
And if, accepting office, the Yahid failed in the punctual and
regular discharge of his duties, he was mulcted and chastised
none the less. A fine of forty pounds drove from the Synagogue
Isaac Disraeli, collector of *Curiosities of Literature,* and made
possible that curiosity of politics, the career of Lord Beaconsfield.
The fathers of the Synagogue, who drew up their constitution in
pure Castilian in the days when Pepys noted the indecorum in
their little Synagogue in King Street, meant their statutes to
cement, not thus to disintegrate, the community. 'Twas a tactless
tyranny, this of the Mohamad, an inelastic administration of a
cast-iron codex wrought "in good King Charles's golden days,"
when the colony of Dutch-Spanish exiles was as a camp in ene-
mies' country, in need of military *régime;* and it co-operated with
the attractions of an unhampered "Christian" career in driving
many a brilliant family beyond the gates of the Ghetto, and into
the pages of Debrett. Athens is always a dangerous rival to
Sparta.

But the Mahamad itself moved strictly in the grooves of pre-
scription. That legalistic instinct of the Hebrew, which had
evolved the most gigantic and minute code of conduct in the

world, had beguiled these latter-day Jews into super-adding to it a local legislation that grew into two hundred pages of Portuguese — an intertangled network of *Ascamot* or regulations, providing for every contingency of Synagogue politics, from the quarrels of members for the best seats down to the dimensions of their graves in the *Carreira*, from the distribution of "good deeds" among the rich to the distribution of Passover Cakes among the poor. If the wheels and pulleys of the communal life moved "by permission of the Mahamad," the Mahamad moved by permission of the *Ascamot*.

The solemn Council was met — "in complete Mahamad." Even the Chief of the Elders was present, by virtue of his privilege, making a sixth; not to count the Chancellor or Secretary, who sat flutteringly fingering the Portuguese Minute Book on the right of the President. He was a little man, an odd medley of pomp and bluster, with a snuff-smeared upper lip, and a nose that had dipped in the wine when it was red. He had a grandiose sense of his own importance, but it was a pride that had its roots in humility, for he felt himself great because he was the servant of greatness. He lived "by permission of the Mahamad." As an official he was theoretically inaccessible. If you approached him on a matter he would put out his palms deprecatingly and pant, "I must consult the Mahamad." It was said of him that he had once been asked the time, and that he had automatically panted, "I must consult the Mahamad." This consultation was the merest form; in practice the Secretary had more influence than the Chief Rabbi, who was not allowed to recommend an applicant for charity for the quaint reason that the respect entertained for him might unduly prejudice the Council in favour of his candidate. As no gentleman of the Mahamad could possibly master the statutes in his year of office, especially as only a rare member understood the Portuguese in which they had been ultimately couched, the Secretary was invariably referred to, for he was permanent, full of saws and precedents, and so he interpreted the law with impartial inaccuracy — "by permission of the Mahamad." In his heart of hearts he believed that the sun rose and the rain fell — "by permission of the Mahamad."

The Council Chamber.was of goodly proportions, and was decorated by gold lettered panels, inscribed with the names of pious donors, thick as saints in a graveyard, overflowing even into the lobby. The flower and chivalry of the Spanish Jewry had sat round that Council-table, grandees who had plumed and ruffled it with the bloods of their day, clanking their swords with the best, punctilious withal and ceremonious, with the stately Castilian courtesy still preserved by the men who were met this afternoon, to whom their memory was as faint as the fading records of the panels. These descendents of theirs had still elaborate salutations and circumlocutions, and austere dignities of debate. "God-fearing men of capacity and respectability," as the *Ascama* demanded, they were also men of money, and it gave them a port and a repose. His Britannic Majesty graced the throne no better than the President of the Mahamad, seated at the head of the long table in his alcoved arm-chair, with the Chief of the Elders on his left, and the Chancellor on his right, and his Councillors all about him. The westering sun sent a pencil of golden light through the Norman windows as if anxious to record the names of those present in gilt letters — "by permission of the Mahamad."

"Let da Costa enter," said the President, when the agenda demanded the great *Schnorrer's* presence.

The Chancellor fluttered to his feet, fussily threw open the door, and beckoned vacancy with his finger till he discovered Manasseh was not in the lobby. The beadle came hurrying up instead.

"Where is da Costa?" panted the Chancellor. "Call da Costa."

"Da Costa!" sonorously intoned the beadle with the long-drawn accent of court ushers.

The corridor rang hollow, empty of Manasseh. "Why, he was here a moment ago," cried the bewildered beadle. He ran down the passage, and found him sure enough at the end of it where it abutted on the street. The King of *Schnorrers* was in dignified converse with a person of consideration.

"Da Costa!" the beadle cried again, but his tone was less awesome and more tetchy. The beggar did not turn his head.

"Mr. da Costa," said the beadle, now arrived too near the imposing figure to venture on familiarities with it. This time the beggar gave indications of restored hearing. "Yes, my man," he said, turning and advancing a few paces to meet the envoy. "Don't go, Grobstock," he called over his shoulder.

"Didn't you hear me calling?" grumbled the beadle.

"I heard you calling da Costa, but I naturally imagined it was one of your drinking companions," replied Manasseh severely.

"The Mahamad is waiting for you," faltered the beadle.

"Tell *the gentlemen* of the Mahamad," said Manasseh, with reproving emphasis, "that I shall do myself the pleasure of being with them presently. Nay, pray don't hurry away, my dear Grobstock," he went on, resuming his place at the German magnate's side — "and so your wife is taking the waters at Tunbridge Wells. In faith, 'tis an excellent regimen for the vapours. I am thinking of sending my wife to Buxton — the warden of our hospital has his country-seat there."

"But you are wanted," murmured Grobstock, who was anxious to escape. He had caught the *Schnorrer's* eye as its owner sunned himself in the archway, and it held him.

" 'Tis only a meeting of the Mahamad I have to attend," he said indifferently. "Rather a nuisance — but duty is duty."

Grobstock's red face became a setting for two expanded eyes.

"I thought the Mahamad was your chief Council," he exclaimed.

"Yes, there are only five of us," said Manasseh lightly, and, while Grobstock gaped incredulous, the Chancellor himself shambled up in pale consternation.

"You are keeping the gentlemen of the Mahamad waiting," he panted imperiously.

"Ah, you are right, Grobstock," said Manasseh with a sigh of resignation. "They cannot get on without me. Well, you will excuse me, I know. I am glad to have seen you again — we shall finish our chat at your house some evening, shall we? I have agreeable recollections of your hospitality."

"My wife will be away all this month," Grobstock repeated feebly.

"Ha! ha! ha!" laughed Manasseh roguishly. "Thank you for the reminder. I shall not fail to aid you in taking advantage of her absence. Perhaps mine will be away, too — at Buxton. Two bachelors, ha! ha! ha!" and, proffering his hand, he shook Grobstock's in gracious farewell. Then he sauntered leisurely in the wake of the feverishly impatient Chancellor, his staff tapping the stones in measured tardiness.

"Good afternoon, gentlemen," he observed affably as he entered the Council Chamber.

"You have kept us waiting," sharply rejoined the President of the Mahamad, ruffled out of his regal suavity. He was a puffy, swarthy personage, elegantly attired, and he leaned forward on his velvet throne, tattooing on the table with bediamonded fingers.

"Not so long as you have kept *me* waiting," said Manasseh with quiet resentment. "If I had known you expected me to cool my heels in the corridor I should not have come, and, had not my friend the Treasurer of the Great Synagogue opportunely turned up to chat with me, I should not have stayed."

"You are impertinent, sir," growled the President.

"I think, sir, it is you who owe me an apology," maintained Manasseh unflinchingly, "and, knowing the courtesy and high breeding which has always distinguished your noble family, I can only explain your present tone by your being unaware I have a grievance. No doubt it is your Chancellor who cited me to appear at too early an hour."

The President, cooled by the quiet dignity of the beggar, turned a questioning glance upon the outraged Chancellor, who was crimson and quivering with confusion and indignation.

"It is usual t-t-to summon persons before the c-c-commencement of the meeting," he stammered hotly. "We cannot tell how long the prior business will take."

"Then I would respectfully submit to the Chief of the Elders," said Manasseh, "that at the next meeting of his august body he move a resolution that persons cited to appear before the Mahamad shall take precedence of all other business."

The Chief of the Elders looked helplessly at the President of the Mahamad, who was equally at sea. "However, I will not press that point now," added Manasseh, "nor will I draw the attention of the committee to the careless, perfunctory manner in which the document summoning me was drawn up, so that, had I been a stickler for accuracy, I need not have answered to the name of Manasseh da Costa."

"But that *is* your name," protested the Chancellor.

"If you will examine the Charity List," said Manasseh magnificently, "you will see that my name is Manasseh Bueno Barzillai Azevedo da Costa. But you are keeping the gentlemen of the Mahamad waiting." And with a magnanimous air of dismissing the past, he seated himself on the nearest empty chair at the foot of the table, leaned his elbows on the table, and his face on his hands, and gazed across at the President immediately opposite. The Councillors were so taken aback by his unexpected bearing that this additional audacity was scarcely noted. But the Chancellor, wounded in his inmost instincts, exclaimed irately, "Stand up, sir. These chairs are for the gentlemen of the Mahamad."

"And being gentlemen," added Manasseh crushingly, "they know better than to keep an old man on his legs any longer."

"If you were a gentleman," retorted the Chancellor, "you would take that thing off your head."

"If you were not a Man-of-the-Earth," rejoined the beggar, "you would know that it is not a mark of disrespect for the Mahamad, but of respect for the Law, which is higher than the Mahamad. The rich man can afford to neglect our holy religion, but the poor man has only the Law. It is his sole luxury."

The pathetic tremor in his voice stirred a confused sense of wrong-doing and injustice in the Councillors' breasts. The President felt vaguely that the edge of his coming impressive rebuke had been turned, if, indeed, he did not sit rebuked instead. Irritated, he turned on the Chancellor, and bade him hold his peace.

"He means well," said Manasseh deprecatingly. "He cannot be expected to have the fine instincts of the gentlemen of the Mahamad. May I ask you, sir," he concluded, "to proceed with the business for which you have summoned me? I have several appointments to keep with clients."

The President's bediamonded fingers recommenced their ill-tempered tattoo; he was fuming inwardly with a sense of baffled wrath, of righteous indignation made unrighteous. "Is it true, sir," he burst forth at last in the most terrible accents he could command in the circumstances, "that you meditate giving your daughter in marriage to a Polish Jew?"

"No," replied Manasseh curtly.

"No?" articulated the President, while a murmur of astonishment went round the table at this unexpected collapse of the whole case.

"Why, your daughter admitted it to my wife," said the Councillor on Manasseh's right.

Manasseh turned to him, expostulant, tilting his chair and body towards him. "My daughter is going to marry a Polish Jew," he explained with argumentative forefinger, "but I do not meditate giving her to him."

"Oh, then, you will refuse your consent," said the Councillor, hitching his chair back so as to escape the beggar's progressive propinquity. "By no means," quoth Manasseh in surprised accents, as he drew his chair nearer again, "I have already consented. I do not *meditate* consenting. That word argues an inconclusive attitude."

"None of your quibbles, sirrah," cried the President, while a scarlet flush mantled on his dark countenance. "Do you know that the union you contemplate is disgraceful and degrading to you, to your daughter, and to the community which has done so much for you? What! A Sephardi marry a Tedesco! Shameful."

"And do you think I do not feel the shame as deeply as you?" enquired Manasseh, with infinite pathos. "Do you think, gentlemen, that I have not suffered from this passion of a Tedesco for my daughter? I came here expecting your sympathy, and do you offer me reproach? Perhaps you think, sir" — here he turned again to his right-hand neighbour, who, in his anxiety to evade his pertinacious proximity, had half-wheeled his chair round, offering only his back to the argumentative forefinger — "perhaps you think, because I have consented, that I cannot condole with you, that I am not at one with you in lamenting this blot on our common 'scutcheon; perhaps you think" — here he adroitly twisted his chair into argumentative position on the other side of the Councillor, rounding him like a cape — "that, because you have no sympathy with my tribulation, I have no sympathy with yours. But, if I have consented, it is only because it was the best I could do for my daughter. In my heart of hearts I have repudiated her, so that she may practically be considered an orphan, and, as such, a fit person to receive the marriage dowry bequeathed by Rodriguez Real, peace be upon him."

"This is no laughing matter, sir," thundered the President, stung into forgetfulness of his dignity by thinking too much of it.

"No, indeed," said Manasseh sympathetically, wheeling to the right so as to confront the President, who went on stormily, "Are you aware, sir, of the penalties you risk by persisting in your course?"

"I risk no penalties," replied the beggar.

"Indeed! Then do you think anyone may trample with impunity upon our ancient *Ascamot?*"

"Our ancient *Ascamot!*" repeated Manasseh in surprise. "What have they to say against a Sephardi marrying a Tedesco?"

The audacity of the question rendered the Council breathless. Manasseh had to answer it himself.

"They have nothing to say. There is no such *Ascama.*" There was a moment of awful silence. It was as though he had disavowed the Decalogue.

"Do you question the first principle of our constitution?" said the President at last, in low, ominous tones. "Do you deny that your daughter is a traitress? Do you — ?"

"Ask your Chancellor," calmly interrupted Manasseh. "He is a Man-of-the-Earth, but he should know your statutes, and he will tell you that my daughter's conduct is nowhere forbidden."

"Silence, sir," cried the President testily. "Mr. Chancellor, read the *Ascama.*"

The Chancellor wriggled on his chair, his face flushing and paling by turns; all eyes were bent upon him in anxious suspense. He hemmed and ha'd and coughed, and took snuff, and blew his nose elaborately.

"There is n-n-no express *Ascama,*" he stuttered at last. Manasseh sat still, in unpretentious triumph.

The Councillor who was now become his right-hand neighbour was the first to break the dazed silence, and it was his first intervention.

"Of course, it was never actually put into writing," he said in stern reproof. "It has never been legislated against, because it has never been conceived possible. These things are an instinct with every right-minded Sephardi. Have we ever legislated against marrying Christians?" Manasseh veered round half a point of the compass, and fixed the new opponent with his argumentative forefinger. "Certainly we have," he replied unexpectedly. "In.Section XX., Paragraph II." He quoted the *Ascama* by heart, rolling out the sonorous Portuguese like a solemn in-

dictment. "If our legislators had intended to prohibit intermar-
riage with the German community, they would have prohibited
it."

"There is the Traditional Law as well as the Written," said
the Chancellor, recovering himself. "It is so in our holy religion,
it is so in our constitution."

"Yes, there are precedents assuredly," cried the President
eagerly.

"There is the case of one of our Treasurers in the time of
George II.," said the little Chancellor, blossoming under the
sunshine of the President's encouragement, and naming the
ancestor of a Duchess of to-day. "He wanted to marry a beautiful
German Jewess."

"And was interdicted," said the President.

"Hem!" coughed the Chancellor. "He — he was only permitted
to marry her under humiliating conditions. The Elders forbade
the attendance of the members of the House of Judgment, or of
the Cantors; no celebration was to take place in the *Snoga;* no
offerings were to be made for the bridegroom's health, nor was
he even to receive the bridegroom's call to the reading of the
Law."

"But the Elders will not impose any such conditions on my
son-in-law," said Manasseh, skirting round another chair so as
to bring his forefinger to play upon the Chief of the Elders, on
whose left he had now arrived in his argumentative advances.
"In the first place he is not one of us. His desire to join us is a
compliment. If anyone has offended your traditions, it is my
daughter. But then she is not a male, like the Treasurer cited;
she is not an active agent, she has not gone out of her way to
choose a Tedesco — she has been chosen. Your masculine precedents cannot touch her."

"Ay, but we can touch you," said the contemporary Treasurer,
guffawing grimly. He sat opposite Manasseh, and next to the
Chancellor.

"Is it fines you are thinking of?" said Manasseh with a scorn-
ful glance across the table. "Very well, fine me — if you can afford it. You know that I am a student, a son of the Law, who
has no resources but what you allow him. If you care to pay this
fine it is your affair. There is always room in the poor-box. I

am always glad to hear of fines. You had better make up your mind to the inevitable, gentlemen. Have I not had to do it? There is no *Ascama* to prevent my son-in-law having all the usual privileges — in fact, it was to ask that he might receive the bridegroom's call to the Law on the Sabbath before his marriage that I really came. By Section III., Paragraph I., you are empowered to admit any person about to marry the daughter of a Yahid." Again the sonorous Portuguese rang out, thrilling the Councillors with all that quintessential awfulness of ancient statutes in a tongue not understood. It was not till a quarter of a century later that the *Ascamot* were translated into English, and from that moment their authority was doomed.

The Chancellor was the first to recover from the quotation. Daily contact with these archaic sanctities had dulled his awe, and the President's impotent irritation spurred him to action.

"But you are *not* a Yahid," he said quietly. "By Paragraph V. of the same section, any one whose name appears on the Charity List ceases to be a Yahid."

"And a vastly proper law," said Manasseh with irony. "Everybody may vote but the *Schnorrer*." And, ignoring the Chancellor's point at great length, he remarked confidentially to the Chief of the Elders, at whose elbow he was still encamped, "It is curious how few of your Elders perceive that those who take the charity are the pillars of the Synagogue. What keeps your community together? Fines. What ensures respect for your constitution? Fines. What makes every man do his duty? Fines. What rules this very Mahamad? Fines. And it is the poor who provide an outlet for all these moneys. Egad, do you think your members would for a moment tolerate your penalties, if they did not know the money was laid out in 'good deeds'? Charity is the salt of riches, says the Talmud, and, indeed, it is the salt that preserves your community."

"Have done, sir, have done!" shouted the President, losing all regard for those grave amenities of the ancient Council Chamber which Manasseh did his best to maintain. "Do you forget to whom you are talking?"

"I am talking to the Chief of the Elders," said Manasseh in a wounded tone, "but if you would like me to address myself to you — " and wheeling round the Chief of the Elders, he landed his chair next to the President's.

"Silence, fellow!" thundered the President, shrinking spasmodically from his confidential contact. "You have no right to a voice at all; as the Chancellor has reminded us, you are not even a Yahid, a congregant."

"Then the laws do not apply to me," retorted the beggar quietly. "It is only the Yahid who is privileged to do this, who is prohibited from doing that. No *Ascama* mentions the *Schnorrer*, or gives you any authority over him."

"On the contrary," said the Chancellor, seeing the President disconcerted again, "he is bound to attend the week-day services. But this man hardly ever does, sir." "I *never* do," corrected Manasseh, with touching sadness. "That is another of the privileges I have to forego in order to take your charity; I cannot risk appearing to my Maker in the light of a mercenary."

"And what prevents you taking your turn in the graveyard watches?" sneered the Chancellor.

The antagonists were now close together, one on either side of the President of the Mahamad, who was wedged between the two bobbing, quarrelling figures, his complexion altering momently for the blacker, and his fingers working nervously.

"What prevents me?" replied Manasseh. "My age. It would be a sin against heaven to spend a night in the cemetery. If the body-snatchers did come they might find a corpse to their hand in the watch-tower. But I do my duty — I always pay a substitute."

"No doubt," said the Treasurer. "I remember your asking me for the money to keep an old man out of the cemetery. Now I see what you meant."

"Yes," began two others, "and I — "

"Order, gentlemen, order," interrupted the President desperately, for the afternoon was flitting, the sun was setting, and the shadows of twilight were falling. "You must not argue with the man. Hark you, my fine fellow, we refuse to sanction this marriage; it shall not be performed by our ministers, nor can we dream of admitting your son-in-law as a Yahid."

"Then admit him on your Charity List," said Manasseh.

"We are more likely to strike *you* off! And, by gad!" cried the President, tattooing on the table with his whole fist, "if you don't stop this scandal instanter, we will send you howling."

"Is it excommunication you threaten?" said Manasseh, rising to his feet. There was a menacing glitter in his eye.

"This scandal must be stopped," repeated the President, agitatedly rising in involuntary imitation.

"Any member of the Mahamad could stop it in a twinkling," said Manasseh sullenly. "You yourself, if you only chose."

"If I only chose?" echoed the President enquiringly.

"If you only chose my daughter. Are you not a bachelor? I am convinced she could not say nay to anyone present — excepting the Chancellor. Only no one is really willing to save the community from this scandal, and so my daughter must marry as best she can. And yet, it is a handsome creature who would not disgrace even a house in Hackney."

Manasseh spoke so seriously that the President fumed the more. "Let her marry this Pole," he ranted, "and you shall be cut off from us in life and death. Alive, you shall worship without our walls, and dead you shall be buried 'behind the boards.' "

"For the poor man — excommunication," said Manasseh in soliloquy. "For the rich man — permission to marry the Tedesco of his choice."

"Leave the room, fellow," vociferated the President. "You have heard our ultimatum!"

But Manasseh did not quail.

"And you shall hear mine," he said, with a quietness that was the more impressive for the President's fury. "Do not forget, Mr. President, that you and I owe allegiance to the same brotherhood. Do not forget that the power which made you can unmake you at the next election; do not forget that if I have no vote I have vast influence; that there is not a Yahid whom I do not visit weekly; that there is not a *Schnorrer* who would not follow me in my exile. Do not forget that there is another community to turn to — yes! that very Ashkenazic community you contemn — with the Treasurer of which I talked but just now; a community that waxes daily in wealth and greatness while you sleep in your sloth." His tall form dominated the chamber, his head seemed to touch the ceiling. The Councillors sat dazed as amid a lightning-storm.

"Jackanapes! Blasphemer! Shameless renegade!" cried the President, choking with wrath. And being already on his legs, he dashed to the bell and tugged at it madly, blanching the Chancellor's face with the perception of a lost opportunity.

"I shall not leave this chamber till I choose," said Manasseh, dropping stolidly into the nearest chair and folding his arms.

At once a cry of horror and consternation rose from every throat, every man leapt threateningly to his feet, and Manasseh realised that he was throned on the alcoved armchair!

But he neither blenched nor budged.

"Nay, keep your seats, gentlemen," he said quietly.

The President, turning at the stir, caught sight of the *Schnorrer*, staggered and clutched at the mantel. The Councillors stood spellbound for an instant, while the Chancellor's eyes roved wildly round the walls, as if expecting the gold names to start from their panels. The beadle rushed in, terrified by the strenuous tintinnabulation, looked instinctively towards the throne for orders, then underwent petrifaction on the threshold, and stared speechless at Manasseh, what time the President, gasping like a landed cod, vainly strove to utter the order for the beggar's expulsion.

"Don't stare at me, Gomez," Manasseh cried imperiously. "Can't you see the President wants a glass of water?"

The beadle darted a glance at the President, and, perceiving his condition, rushed out again to get the water.

This was the last straw. To see his authority usurped as well as his seat maddened the poor President. For some seconds he strove to mouth an oath, embracing his supine Councillors as well as this beggar on horseback, but he produced only an inarticulate raucous cry, and reeled sideways. Manasseh sprang from his chair and caught the falling form in his arms. For one terrible moment he stood supporting it in a tense silence, broken only by the incoherent murmurs of the unconscious lips; then crying angrily, "Bestir yourselves, gentlemen, don't you see the President is ill?" he dragged his burden towards the table, and, aided by the panic-stricken Councillors, laid it flat thereupon, and threw open the ruffled shirt. He swept the Minute Book to the floor with an almost malicious movement, to make room for the President.

The beadle returned with the glass of water, which he wellnigh dropped.

"Run for a physician," Manasseh commanded, and throwing away the water carelessly, in the Chancellor's direction, he asked if anyone had any brandy. There was no response.

"Come, come, Mr. Chancellor," he said, "bring out your phial." And the abashed functionary obeyed.

"Has any of you his equipage without?" Manasseh demanded next of the Mahamad.

They had not, so Manasseh despatched the Chief of the Elders in quest of a sedan chair. Then there was nothing left but to await the physician.

"You see, gentlemen, how insecure is earthly power," said the *Schnorrer* solemnly, while the President breathed stertorously, deaf to his impressive moralising. "It is swallowed up in an instant, as Lisbon was engulfed. Cursed are they who despise the poor. How is the saying of our sages verified — 'The house that opens not to the poor opens to the physician.'" His eyes shone with unearthly radiance in the gathering gloom.

The cowed assembly wavered before his words, like reeds before the wind, or conscience-stricken kings before fearless prophets.

When the physician came he pronounced that the President had had a slight stroke of apoplexy, involving a temporary paralysis of the right foot. The patient, by this time restored to consciousness, was conveyed home in the sedan chair, and the Mahamad dissolved in confusion. Manasseh was the last to leave the Council Chamber. As he stalked into the corridor he turned the key in the door behind him with a vindictive twist. Then, plunging his hand into his breeches-pocket, he gave the beadle a crown, remarking genially, "You must have your usual perquisite, I suppose."

The beadle was moved to his depths. He had a burst of irresistible honesty. "The President gives me only half-a-crown," he murmured.

"Yes, but he may not be able to attend the next meeting," said Manasseh. "And I may be away, too."

CHAPTER VI

SHOWING HOW THE KING ENRICHED THE SYNAGOGUE

THE Synagogue of the Gates of Heaven was crowded — members, orphan boys, *Schnorrers,* all were met in celebration of the Sabbath. But the President of the Mahamad was missing. He was still inconvenienced by the effects of his stroke, and deemed it most prudent to pray at home. The Council of Five had not met since Manasseh had dissolved it, and so the matter of his daughter's marriage was left hanging, as indeed was not seldom the posture of matters discussed by Sephardic bodies. The authorities thus passive, Manasseh found scant difficulty in imposing his will upon the minor officers, less ready than himself with constitutional precedent. His daughter was to be married under the Sephardic canopy, and no jot of synagogual honour was to be bated the bridegroom. On this Sabbath — the last before the wedding — Yankelé was to be called to the Reading of the Law . like a true-born Portuguese. He made his first appearance in the Synagogue of his bride's fathers with a feeling of solemn respect, not exactly due to Manasseh's grandiose references to the ancient temple. He had walked the courtyard with levity, half prepared, from previous experience of his intended father-in-law, to find the glories insubstantial. Their unexpected actuality awed him, and he was glad he was dressed in his best. His beaver hat, green trousers, and brown coat equalled him with the massive pillars, the gleaming candelabra, and the stately roof. Da Costa, for his part, had made no change in his attire; he dignified his shabby vestments, stuffing them with royal manhood, and wearing his snuff-coloured over-garment like a purple robe. There was, in

sooth, an official air about his habiliment, and to the worshippers it was as impressively familiar as the black stole and white
bands of the Cantor. It seemed only natural that he should be
called to the Reading first, quite apart from the fact that he was
a *Cohen*, of the family of Aaron, the High Priest, a descent that,
perhaps, lent something to the loftiness of his carriage.

When the Minister intoned vigorously, "The good name,
Manasseh, the son of Judah, the Priest, the man, shall arise to
read in the Law," every eye was turned with a new interest on
the prospective father-in-law. Manasseh arose composedly, and,
hitching his sliding prayer-shawl over his left shoulder, stalked
to the reading platform, where he chanted the blessings with imposing flourishes, and stood at the Minister's right hand while
his section of the Law was read from the sacred scroll. There
was many a man of figure in the congregation, but none who
became the platform better. It was beautiful to see him pay his
respects to the scroll; it reminded one of the meeting of two
sovereigns. The great moment, however, was when, the section
being concluded, the Master Reader announced Manasseh's
donations to the Synagogue. The financial statement was in-
corporated in a long Benediction, like a coin wrapped up in
folds of paper. This was always a great moment, even when in-
considerable personalities were concerned, each man's generosity
being the subject of speculation before and comment after. Manasseh, it was felt, would, although a mere *Schnorrer*, rise to the
height of the occasion, and offer as much as seven and sixpence.
The shrewder sort suspected he would split it up into two or
three separate offerings, to give an air of inexhaustible largess.

The shrewder sort were right and wrong, as is their habit.

The Master Reader began his quaint formula, "May He who
blessed our Fathers," pausing at the point where the Hebrew is
blank for the amount. He span out the prefatory "Who vows"
— the last note prolonging itself, like the vibration of a tuning-
fork, at a literal pitch of suspense. It was a sensational halt,
due to his forgetting the amounts or demanding corroboration
at the eleventh hour, and the stingy often recklessly amended
their contributions, panic-struck under the pressure of imminent
publicity.

"Who vows — " The congregation hung upon his lips. With
his usual gesture of interrogation, he inclined his ear towards

Manasseh's mouth, his face wearing an unusual look of perplexity; and those nearest the platform were aware of a little colloquy between the *Schnorrer* and the Master Reader, the latter bewildered and agitated, the former stately. The delay had discomposed the Master as much as it had whetted the curiosity of the congregation. He repeated:

"Who vows — *cinco livras*" — he went on glibly without a pause — "for charity — for the life of Yankov ben Yitzchok, his son-in-law, &c., &c." But few of the worshippers heard any more than the *cinco livras* (five pounds). A thrill ran through the building. Men pricked up their ears, incredulous, whispering one another. One man deliberately moved from his place towards the box in which sat the Chief of the Elders, the presiding dignitary in the absence of the President of the Mahamad.

"I didn't catch — how much was that?" he asked.

"Five pounds," said the Chief of the Elders shortly. He suspected an irreverent irony in the Beggar's contribution.

The Benediction came to an end, but ere the hearers had time to realise the fact, the Master Reader had started on another. "May He who blessed our fathers!" he began, in the strange traditional recitative. The wave of curiosity mounted again, higher than before.

"Who vows — "

The wave hung an instant, poised and motionless.

"Cinco livras!"

The wave broke in a low murmur, amid which the Master imperturbably proceeded, "For oil — for the life of his daughter Deborah, &c." When he reached the end there was a poignant silence.

Was it to be *da capo* again?

"May He who blessed our fathers!"

The wave of curiosity surged once more, rising and subsiding with this ebb and flow of financial Benediction.

"Who vows — *cinco livras* — for the wax candles."

This time the thrill, the whisper, the flutter, swelled into a positive buzz. The gaze of the entire congregation was focussed upon the Beggar, who stood impassive in the blaze of glory. Even the orphan boys, packed in their pew, paused in their inattention to the Service, and craned their necks towards the platform. The veriest magnates did not thus play piety with five

pound points. In the ladies' gallery the excitement was intense.
The occupants gazed eagerly through the grille. One woman —
a buxom dame of forty summers, richly clad and jewelled — had
risen, and was tiptoeing frantically over the woodwork, her
feather waving like a signal of distress. It was Manasseh's wife.
The waste of money maddened her, each donation hit her like
a poisoned arrow; in vain she strove to catch her spouse's eye.
The air seemed full of gowns and toques and farthingales flam-
ing away under her very nose, without her being able to move
hand or foot in rescue; whole wardrobes perished at each Benediction. It was with the utmost difficulty she restrained herself
from shouting down to her prodigal lord. At her side the radiant
Deborah vainly tried to pacify her by assurances that Manasseh
never intended to pay up.

"Who vows — " The Benediction had begun for a fourth time.

"*Cinco livras* for the Holy Land." And the sensation grew.
"For the life of this holy congregation, &c."

The Master Reader's voice droned on impassively, intermin-
ably.

The fourth Benediction was drawing to its close, when the
beadle was seen to mount the platform and whisper in his ear.
Only Manasseh overheard the message.

"The Chief of the Elders says you must stop. This is mere
mockery. The man is a *Schnorrer,* an impudent beggar."

The beadle descended the steps, and after a moment of inau-
dible discussion with da Costa, the Master Reader lifted up his
voice afresh.

The Chief of the Elders frowned and clenched his praying-
shawl angrily. It was a fifth Benediction! But the Reader's sing-
song went on, for Manasseh's wrath was nearer than the magnate's.

"Who vows — *cinco livras* — for the Captives — for the life of
the Chief of the Elders!"

The Chief bit his lip furiously at this delicate revenge; galled
almost to frenzy by the aggravating foreboding that the congregation would construe his message as a solicitation of the
polite attention. For it was of the amenities of the Synagogue for
rich people to present these Benedictions to one another. And
so the endless stream of donatives flowed on, provoking the
hearers to fever pitch. The very orphan boys forgot that this

prolongation of the service was retarding their breakfasts indefinitely. Every warden, dignitary and official, from the President of the Mahamad down to the very Keeper of the Bath, was honoured by name in a special Benediction, the chief of Manasseh's weekly patrons were repaid almost in kind on this unique and festive occasion. Most of the congregation kept count of the sum total, which was mounting, mounting . . . .

Suddenly there was a confusion in the ladies' gallery, cries, a babble of tongues. The beadle hastened upstairs to impose his authority. The rumour circulated that Mrs. da Costa had fainted and been carried out. It reached Manasseh's ears, but he did not move. He stood at his post, unfaltering, donating, blessing.

"Who vows — *cinco livras* — for the life of his wife, Sarah!" And a faint sardonic smile flitted across the Beggar's face.

The oldest worshipper wondered if the record would be broken. Manasseh's benefactions were approaching thrillingly near the highest total hitherto reached by any one man upon any one occasion. Every brain was troubled by surmises. The Chief of the Elders, fuming impotently, was not alone in apprehending a blasphemous mockery; but the bulk imagined that the *Schnorrer* had come into property or had always been a man of substance, and was now taking this means of restoring to the Synagogue the funds he had drawn from it. And the fountain of Benevolence played on.

The record figure was reached and left in the rear. When at length the poor Master Reader, sick unto death of the oft-repeated formula (which might just as well have covered all the contributions the first time, though Manasseh had commanded each new Benediction as if by an after-thought), was allowed to summon the Levite who succeeded Manasseh, the Synagogue had been enriched by a hundred pounds. The last Benediction had been coupled with the name of the poorest *Schnorrer* present — an assertion and glorification of Manasseh's own order that put the coping-stone on this sensational memorial of the Royal Wedding. It was, indeed, a kingly munificence, a sovereign graciousness. Nay, before the Service was over, Manasseh even begged the Chief of the Elders to permit a special *Rogation* to be said for a sick person. The Chief, meanly snatching at this opportunity of reprisals, refused, till, learning that Manasseh alluded to the ailing President of the Mahamad, he collapsed ingloriously.

But the real hero of the day was Yankelé, who shone chiefly by reflected light, but yet shone even more brilliantly than the Spaniard, for to him was added the double lustre of the bridegroom and the stranger, and he was the cause and centre of the sensation.

His eyes twinkled continuously throughout.

The next day, Manasseh fared forth to collect the hundred pounds!

The day being Sunday, he looked to find most of his clients at home. He took Grobstock first as being nearest, but the worthy speculator and East India Director espied him from an upper window, and escaped by a back-door into Goodman's Fields — a prudent measure, seeing that the incredulous Manasseh ransacked the house in quest of him. Manasseh's manner was always a search-warrant.

The King consoled himself by paying his next visit to a personage who could not possibly evade him — none other than the sick President of the Mahamad. He lived in Devonshire Square, in solitary splendour. Him Manasseh bearded in his library, where the convalescent was sorting his collection of prints. The visitor had had himself announced as a gentleman on synagogual matters, and the public-spirited President had not refused himself to the business. But when he caught sight of Manasseh, his puffy features were distorted, he breathed painfully, and put his hand to his hip.

"You!" he gasped.

"Have a care, my dear sir! Have a care!" said Manasseh anxiously, as he seated himself. "You are still weak. To come to the point — for I would not care to distract too much a man indispensable to the community, who has already felt the hand of the Almighty for his treatment of the poor — "

He saw that his words were having effect, for these prosperous pillars of the Synagogue were mightily superstitious under affliction, and he proceeded in gentler tones. "To come to the point, it is my duty to inform you (for I am the only man who is certain of it) that while you have been away our Synagogue has made a bad debt!"

"A bad debt!" An angry light leapt into the President's eyes. There had been an ancient practice of lending out the funds to members, and the President had always set his face against the survival of the policy. "It would not have been made had I been there!" he cried.

"No, indeed," admitted Manasseh. "You would have stopped it in its early stages. The Chief of the Elders tried, but failed."

"The dolt!" cried the President. "A man without a backbone. How much is it?"

"A hundred pounds!"

"A hundred pounds!" echoed the President, seriously concerned at this blot upon his year of office. "And who is the debtor?"

"I am."

"You! You have borrowed a hundred pounds, you — you jackanapes!"

"Silence, sir! How dare you? I should leave this apartment at once, were it not that I cannot go without your apology. Never in my life have I borrowed a hundred pounds — nay, never have I borrowed one farthing. I am no borrower. If you are a gentleman, you will apologise!"

"I am sorry if I misunderstood," murmured the poor President, "but how, then, do you owe the money?"

"How, then?" repeated Manasseh impatiently. "Cannot you understand that I have donated it to the Synagogue?"

The President stared at him open-mouthed.

"I vowed it yesterday in celebration of my daughter's marriage."

The President let a sigh of relief pass through his open mouth. He was even amused a little.

"Oh, is that all? It was like your deuced effrontery; but still, the Synagogue doesn't lose anything. There's no harm done."

"What is that you say?" enquired Manasseh sternly. "Do you mean to say I am not to pay this money?"

"How can you?"

"How can I? I come to you and others like you to pay it for me."

"Nonsense! Nonsense!" said the President, beginning to lose his temper again. "We'll let it pass. There's no harm done."

"And this is the President of the Mahamad!" soliloquised the *Schnorrer* in bitter astonishment. "This is the chief of our ancient, godly Council! What, sir! Do you hold words spoken solemnly in Synagogue of no account? Would you have me break my solemn vow? Do you wish to bring the Synagogue institutions into contempt? Do you — a man already once stricken by Heaven — invite its chastisement again?"

The President had grown pale — his brain was reeling.

"Nay, ask its forgiveness, sir," went on the King implacably; "and make good this debt of mine in token of your remorse, as it is written, 'And repentance, and prayer, and *charity* avert the evil decree.' "

"Not a penny!" cried the President, with a last gleam of lucidity, and strode furiously towards the bell-pull. Then he stood still in sudden recollection of a similar scene in the Council Chamber.

"You need not trouble to ring for a stroke," said Manasseh grimly. "Then the Synagogue is to be profaned, then even the Benediction which I in all loyalty and forgiveness caused to be said for the recovery of the President of the Mahamad is to be null, a mockery in the sight of the Holy One, blessed be He!"

The President tottered into his reading-chair.

"How much did you vow on my behalf?"

"Five pounds."

The President precipitately drew out a pocket-book and extracted a crisp Bank of England note.

"Give it to the Chancellor," he breathed, exhausted.

"I am punished," quoth Manasseh plaintively as he placed it in his bosom. "I should have vowed ten for you." And he bowed himself out.

In like manner did he collect other contributions that day from Sephardic celebrities, pointing out that now a foreign Jew — Yankelé to wit — had been admitted to their communion, it behoved them to show themselves at their best. What a bad effect it would have on Yankelé if a Sephardi was seen to vow with impunity! First impressions were everything, and they could not be too careful. It would not do for Yankelé to circulate contumelious reports of them among his kin. Those who remonstrated with him over his extravagance he reminded that he had only one daughter, and he drew their attention to the favourable influence his example had had on the Saturday receipts. Not a man of those who came after him in the Reading had ventured to offer half-crowns. He had fixed the standard in gold for that day at least, and who knew what noble emulation he had fired for the future?

Every man who yielded to Manasseh's eloquence was a step to reach the next, for Manasseh made a list of donors, and paraded it reproachfully before those who had yet to give. Withal, the most obstinate resistance met him in some quarters. One man — a certain Rodriques, inhabiting a mansion in Finsbury Circus — was positively rude.

"If I came in a carriage, you'd soon pull out your ten-pound note for the Synagogue," sneered Manasseh, his blood boiling.

"Certainly I would," admitted Rodriques laughing. And Manasseh shook off the dust of his threshold in disdain.

By reason of such rebuffs, his collection for the day only reached about thirty pounds, inclusive of the value of some depreciated Portuguese bonds which he good-naturedly accepted as though at par.

Disgusted with the meanness of mankind, da Costa's genius devised more drastic measures. Having carefully locked up the proceeds of Sunday's operations, and, indeed, nearly all his loose cash, in his safe, for, to avoid being put to expense, he rarely carried money on his person, unless he gathered it *en route*, he took his way to Bishopsgate Within, to catch the stage for Clapton. The day was bright, and he hummed a festive Synagogue tune as he plodded leisurely with his stick along the bustling, narrow pavements, bordered by costers' barrows at one edge, and by jagged houses, overhung by grotesque signboards, at the other, and thronged by cits in worsted hose.

But when he arrived at the inn he found the coach had started. Nothing concerned, he ordered a post-chaise in a supercilious manner, criticising the horses, and drove to Clapton in style, drawn by a pair of spanking steeds, to the music of the postillion's horn. Very soon they drew out of the blocked roads, with their lumbering procession of carts, coaches, and chairs, and into open country, green with the fresh verdure of the spring. The chaise stopped at "The Red Cottage," a pretty villa, whose façade was covered with Virginian creeper that blushed in the autumn. Manasseh was surprised at the taste with which the lawn was laid out in the Italian style, with grottoes and marble figures. The householder, hearing the windings of the horn, conceived himself visited by a person of quality, and sent a message that he was in the hands of his hairdresser, but would be down in less than half an hour. This was of a piece with Manasseh's information concerning the man — a certain Belasco, emulous of the great fops, an amateur of satin waistcoats and novel shoestrings, and even said to affect a spying-glass when he showed at Vauxhall. Manasseh had never seen him, not having troubled to go so far afield, but from the handsome appurtenances of the hall and the staircase he augured the best. The apartments were even more to his liking; they were oak panelled, and crammed with the most expensive objects of art and luxury. The walls of the drawing-room were frescoed, and from the ceiling depended a brilliant lustre, with seven spouts for illumination.

Having sufficiently examined the furniture, Manasseh grew weary of waiting, and betook himself to Belasco's bed-chamber.

"You will excuse me, Mr. Belasco," he said, as he entered through the half open door, "but my business is urgent."

The young dandy, who was seated before a mirror, did not look up, but replied, "Have a care, sir, you well nigh startled my hairdresser."

"Far be it from me to willingly discompose an artist," replied Manasseh drily, "though from the elegance of the design, I venture to think my interruption will not make a hair's-breadth of difference. But I come on a matter which the son of Benjamin Belasco will hardly deny is more pressing than his toilette."

"Nay, nay, sir, what can be more momentous?"

"The Synagogue!" said Manasseh austerely.

"Pah! What are you talking of, sir?" and he looked up cautiously for the first time at the picturesque figure. "What does the Synagogue want of me? I pay my *finta* and every bill the rascals send me. Monstrous fine sums, too, egad — "

"But you never go there!"

"No, indeed, a man of fashion cannot be everywhere. Routs and ridotti play the deuce with one's time."

"What a pity!" mused Manasseh ironically. "One misses you there. 'Tis no edifying spectacle — a slovenly rabble with none to set the standard of taste."

The pale-faced beau's eyes lit up with a gleam of interest.

"Ah, the clods!" he said. "You should yourself be a buck of

the eccentric school by your dress. But I stick to the old tradition of elegance."

"You had better stick to the old tradition of piety," quoth Manasseh. "Your father was a saint, you are a sinner in Israel. Return to the Synagogue, and herald your return by contributing to its finances. It has made a bad debt, and I am collecting money to reimburse it."

The young exquisite yawned. "I know not who you may be," he said at length, "but you are evidently not one of us. As for the Synagogue I am willing to reform its dress, but dem'd if I will give a shilling more to its finances. Let your slovenly rabble of tradesmen pay the piper — I cannot afford it!"

"You cannot afford it!"

"No — you see I have such extravagant tastes."

"But I give you the opportunity for extravagance," expostulated Manasseh. "What greater luxury is there than that of doing good?"

"Confound it, sir, I must ask you to go," said Beau Belasco coldly. "Do you not perceive that you are disconcerting my hairdresser?"

"I could not abide a moment longer under this profane, if tasteful, roof," said Manasseh, backing sternly towards the door. "But I would make one last appeal to you, for the sake of the repose of your father's soul, to forsake your evil ways."

"Be hanged to you for a meddler," retorted the young blood. "My money supports men of genius and taste — it shall not be frittered away on a pack of fusty shopkeepers."

The *Schnorrer* drew himself up to his full height, his eyes darted fire. "Farewell, then!" he hissed in terrible tones. *"You will make the third at Grace!"*

He vanished — the dandy started up full of vague alarm, forgetting even his hair in the mysterious menace of that terrifying sibilation.

"What do you mean?" he cried.

"I mean," said Manasseh, reappearing at the door, "that since the world was created, only two men have taken their clothes with them to the world to come. One was Korah, who was swallowed down, the other was Elijah, who was borne aloft. It is patent in which direction the third will go."

The sleeping chord of superstition vibrated under Manasseh's dexterous touch.

"Rejoice, O young man, in your strength," went on the Beggar, "but a day will come when only the corpse-watchers will perform your toilette. In plain white they will dress you, and the devil shall never know what a dandy you were."

"But who are you, that I should give you money for the Synagogue?" asked the Beau sullenly. "Where are your credentials?"

"Was it to insult me that you called me back? Do I look a knave? Nay, put up your purse. I'll have none of your filthy gold. Let me go."

Gradually Manasseh was won round to accepting ten sovereigns.

"For your father's sake," he said, pocketing them. "The only thing I will take for your sake is the cost of my conveyance. I had to post hither, and the Synagogue must not be the loser."

Beau Belasco gladly added the extra money, and reseated himself before the mirror, with agreeable sensations in his neglected conscience. "You see," he observed, half apologetically, for Manasseh still lingered, "one cannot do everything. To be a prince of dandies, one needs all one's time." He waved his hand comprehensively around the walls which were lined with wardrobes. "My buckskin breeches were the result of nine separate measurings. Do you note how they fit?"

"They scarcely do justice to your eminent reputation," replied Manasseh candidly.

Beau Belasco's face became whiter than even at the thought of earthquakes and devils. "They fit me to bursting!" he breathed.

"But are they in the pink of fashion?" queried Manasseh. "And assuredly the nankeen pantaloons yonder I recollect to have seen worn last year."

"My tailor said they were of a special cut — 'tis a shape I am introducing, baggy — to go with frilled shirts."

Manasseh shook his head sceptically, whereupon the Beau besought him to go through his wardrobe, and set aside anything that lacked originality or extreme fashionableness. After considerable reluctance Manasseh consented, and set aside a few cravats, shirts, periwigs, and suits from the immense collection.

"Aha! That is all you can find," said the Beau gleefully.

"Yes, that is all," said Manasseh sadly. "All I can find that does any justice to your fame. These speak the man of polish and invention; the rest are but tawdry frippery. Anybody might wear them."

"Anybody!" gasped the poor Beau, stricken to the soul.

"Yes, I might wear them myself."

"Thank you! Thank you! You are an honest man. I love true criticism, when the critic has nothing to gain. I am delighted you called. These rags shall go to my valet."

"Nay, why waste them on the heathen?" asked Manasseh, struck with a sudden thought. "Let me dispose of them for the benefit of the Synagogue."

"If it would not be troubling you too much!"

"Is there anything I would not do for Heaven?" said Manasseh with a patronising air. He threw open the door of the adjoining piece suddenly, disclosing the scowling valet on his knees. "Take these down, my man," he said quietly, and the valet was only too glad to hide his confusion at being caught eavesdropping by hastening down to the drive with an armful of satin waistcoats.

Manasseh, getting together the remainder, shook his head despairingly. "I shall never get these into the post-chaise," he said. "You will have to lend me your carriage."

"Can't you come back for them?" said the Beau feebly.

"Why waste the Synagogue's money on hired vehicles? No, if you will crown your kindness by sending the footman along with me to help unpack them, you shall have your equipage back in an hour or two."

So the carriage and pair were brought out, and Manasseh, pressing into his service the coachman, the valet, and the footman, superintended the packing of the bulk of Beau Belasco's wardrobe into the two vehicles. Then he took his seat in the carriage, the coachman and the gorgeous powdered footman got into their places, and with a joyous fanfaronade on the horn, the procession set off, Manasseh bowing graciously to the master of "The Red House," who was waving his beruffled hand from a window embowered in greenery. After a pleasant drive, the vehicles halted at the house, guarded by stone lions, in which dwelt Nathaniel Furtado, the wealthy private dealer, who willingly gave fifteen pounds for the buck's belaced and embroidered vestments, besides being inveigled into a donation of a guinea towards the Synagogue's bad debt. Manasseh thereupon dismissed

the chaise with a handsome gratuity, and drove in state in the
now-empty carriage, attended by the powdered footman, to Finsbury Circus, to the mansion of Rodriques. "I have come for my
ten pounds," he said, and reminded him of his promise (?).
Rodriques laughed, and swore, and laughed again, and swore
that the carriage was hired, to be paid for out of the ten pounds.

"Hired?" echoed Manasseh resentfully. "Do you not recognize
the arms of my friend, Beau Belasco?" And he presently drove
off with the note, for Rodriques had a roguish eye. And then,
parting with the chariot, the King took his way on foot to Fenchurch Street, to the house of his cousin Barzillai, the ex-planter
of Barbadoes, and now a West Indian merchant.

Barzillai, fearing humiliation before his clerks, always carried
his relative off to the neighbouring Franco's Head Tavern, and
humoured him with costly liquors.

"But you had no right to donate money you did not possess;
it was dishonest," he cried with irrepressible ire.

"Hoity toity!" said Manasseh, setting down his glass so vehemently that the stem shivered. "And were you not called to
the Law after me? And did you not donate money?"

"Certainly! But I *had* the money."

"What! *With* you?"

"No, no, certainly not. I do not carry money on the Sabbath."

"Exactly. Neither do I."

"But the money was at my bankers'."

"And so it was at mine. *You* are my bankers, you and others
like you. You draw on your bankers — I draw on mine." And his
cousin being thus confuted, Manasseh had not much further
difficulty in wheedling two pounds ten out of him.

"And now," said he, "I really think you ought to do something
to lessen the Synagogue's loss."

"But I have just given!" quoth Barzillai in bewilderment.

"*That* you gave to me as your cousin, to enable your relative
to discharge his obligations. I put it strictly on a personal foot-
ing. But now I am pleading on behalf of the Synagogue, which
stands to lose heavily. You are a Sephardi as well as my cousin.
It is a distinction not unlike the one I have so often to explain
to you. You owe me charity, not only as a cousin, but as a
Schnorrer likewise." And, having wrested another guinea from

the obfuscated merchant, he repaired to Grobstock's business office in search of the defaulter.

But the wily Grobstock, forewarned by Manasseh's promise to visit him, and further frightened by his Sunday morning call, had denied himself to the *Schnorrer* or anyone remotely resembling him, and it was not till the afternoon that Manasseh ran him to earth at Sampson's coffee-house in Exchange Alley, where the brokers foregathered, and 'prentices and students swaggered in to abuse the Ministers, and all kinds of men from bloods to barristers loitered to pick up hints to easy riches. Manasseh detected his quarry in the furthermost box, his face hidden behind a broadsheet.

"Why do you always come to me?" muttered the East India Director helplessly.

"Eh?" said Manasseh, mistrustful of his own ears. "I beg your pardon."

"If your own community cannot support you," said Grobstock, more loudly, and with all the boldness of an animal driven to bay, "why not go to Abraham Goldsmid, or his brother Ben, or to Van Oven, or Oppenheim — they're all more prosperous than I."

"Sir!" said Manasseh wrathfully. "You are a skilful — nay, a famous, financier. You know what stocks to buy, what stocks to sell, when to follow a rise, and when a fall. When the Premier advertises the loans, a thousand speculators look to you for guidance. What would you say if *I* presumed to interfere in your financial affairs — if I told you to issue these shares or to call in those? You would tell me to mind my own business; and you would be perfectly right. Now *Schnorring* is *my* business. Trust me, I know best whom to come to. You stick to stocks and leave *Schnorring* alone. You are the King of Financiers, but I am the King of *Schnorrers*."

Grobstock's resentment at the rejoinder was mitigated by the compliment to his financial insight. To be put on the same level with the Beggar was indeed unexpected.

"Will you have a cup of coffee?" he said.

"I ought scarcely to drink with you after your reception of me," replied Manasseh unappeased. "It is not even as if I came to *schnorr* for myself; it is to the finances of our house of worship that I wished to give you an opportunity of contributing."

"Aha! your vaunted community hard up?" queried Joseph, with a complacent twinkle.

"Sir! We are the richest congregation in the world. We want nothing from anybody," indignantly protested Manasseh, as he absent-mindedly took the cup of coffee which Grobstock had ordered for him. "The difficulty merely is that, in honour of my daughter's wedding, I have donated a hundred pounds to the Synagogue which I have not yet managed to collect, although I have already devoted a day-and-a-half of my valuable time to the purpose."

"But why do you come to me?"

"What! Do you ask me that again?"

"I — I — mean," stammered Grobstock — "why should I contribute to a Portuguese Synagogue?"

Manasseh clucked his tongue in despair of such stupidity. "It is just you who should contribute more than any Portuguese."

"I?" Grobstock wondered if he was awake.

"Yes, you. Was not the money spent in honour of the marriage of a German Jew? It was a splendid vindication of your community."

"This is too much!" cried Grobstock, outraged and choking.

"Too much to mark the admission to our fold of the first of your sect! I am disappointed in you, deeply disappointed. I thought you would have applauded my generous behaviour."

"I don't care what you thought!" gasped Grobstock. He was genuinely exasperated at the ridiculousness of the demand, but he was also pleased to find himself preserving so staunch a front against the insidious *Schnorrer*. If he could only keep firm now, he told himself, he might emancipate himself for ever. Yes, he would be strong, and Manasseh should never dare address him again. "I won't pay a stiver," he roared.

"If you make a scene I will withdraw," said Manasseh quietly. "Already there are ears and eyes turned upon you. From your language people will be thinking me a dun and you a bankrupt."

"They can go to the devil!" thundered Grobstock, "and you too!"

"Blasphemer! You counsel me to ask the devil to contribute to the Synagogue! I will not bandy words with you. You refuse, then, to contribute to this fund?"

"I do, I see no reason."

"Not even the five pounds I vowed on behalf of Yankelé himself — one of your own people?"

"What! I pay in honour of Yankelé — a dirty *Schnorrer!*"

"Is this the way you speak of your guests?" said Manasseh, in pained astonishment. "Do you forget that Yankelé has broken bread at your table? Perhaps this is how you talk of me when my back is turned. But, beware! Remember the saying of our sages, 'You and I cannot live in the world,' said God to the haughty man. Come, now! No more paltering or taking refuge in abuse. You refuse me this beggarly five pounds?"

"Most decidedly."

"Very well, then!"

Manasseh called the attendant.

"What are you about to do?" cried Grobstock apprehensively.

"You shall see," said Manasseh resolutely, and when the attendant came, he pressed the price of his cup of coffee into his hand.

Grobstock flushed in silent humiliation. Manasseh rose.

Grobstock's fatal strain of weakness gave him a twinge of compunction at the eleventh hour.

"You see for yourself how unreasonable your request was," he murmured.

"Do not strive to justify yourself, I am done with you," said Manasseh. "I am done with you as a philanthropist. For the future you may besnuff and bespatter your coat as much as you please, for all the trouble I shall ever take. As a financier, I still respect you, and may yet come to you, but as a philanthropist, never."

"Anything I can do — " muttered Grobstock vaguely.

"Let me see!" said Manasseh, looking down upon him thoughtfully. "Ah, yes, an idea! I have collected over sixty pounds. If you would invest this for me — "

"Certainly, certainly," interrupted Grobstock, with conciliatory eagerness.

"Good! With your unrivalled knowledge of the markets, you could easily bring it up to the necessary sum in a day or two. Perhaps even there is some grand *coup* on the *tapis*, something to be bulled or beared in which you have a hand."

Grobstock nodded his head vaguely. He had already remembered that the proceeding was considerably below his dignity; he was not a stockbroker, never had he done anything of the kind for anyone.

"But suppose I lose it all?" he asked, trying to draw back.

"Impossible," said the *Schnorrer* serenely. "Do you forget it is a Synagogue fund? Do you think the Almighty will suffer His money to be lost?"

"Then why not speculate yourself?" said Grobstock craftily.

"The Almighty's honour must be guarded. What! Shall He be less well served than an earthly monarch? Do you think I do not know your financial relations with the Court? The service of the Almighty demands the best men. I was the best man to collect the money — you are the best to invest it. To-morrow morning it shall be in your hands."

"No, don't trouble," said Grobstock feebly. "I don't need the actual money to deal with."

"I thank you for your trust in me," replied Manasseh with emotion. "Now you speak like yourself again. I withdraw what I said to you. I *will* come to you again — to the philanthropist no less than financier. And — and I am sorry I paid for my coffee." His voice quivered.

Grobstock was touched. He took out a sixpence and repaid his guest with interest. Manasseh slipped the coin into his pocket, and shortly afterwards, with some final admonitions to his stock-jobber, took his leave.

Being in for the job, Grobstock resolved to make the best of it. His latent vanity impelled him to astonish the Beggar. It happened that he *was* on the point of magnificent manœuvre, and alongside his own triton Manasseh's minnow might just as well swim. He made the sixty odd pounds into six hundred.

A few days after the Royal Wedding, the glories of which are still a tradition among the degenerate *Schnorrers* of to-day, Manasseh struck the Chancellor breathless by handing him a bag containing five score of sovereigns. Thus did he honourably fulfil his obligation to the Synagogue, and with more celerity than many a Warden. Nay, more! Justly considering the results of the speculation should accrue to the Synagogue, whose money had been risked, he, with Quixotic scrupulousness, handed over the balance of five hundred pounds to the Mahamad, stipulating only that it should be used to purchase a life-annuity (styled the Da Costa Fund) for a poor and deserving member of the congregation, in whose selection he, as donor, should have the ruling voice. The Council of Five eagerly agreed to his conditions, and a special junta was summoned for the election. The donor's choice fell upon Manasseh Bueno Barbillai Azevedo da Costa, thenceforward universally recognised, and hereby handed down to tradition, as the King of *Schnorrers*.

A CATALOG OF SELECTED DOVER
BOOKS IN ALL FIELDS OF INTEREST

CONCERNING THE SPIRITUAL IN ART, Wassily Kandinsky. Pioneering work by father of abstract art. Thoughts on color theory, nature of art. Analysis of earlier masters. 12 illustrations. 80pp. of text. 5⅜ x 8½.   23411-8

ANIMALS: 1,419 Copyright-Free Illustrations of Mammals, Birds, Fish, Insects, etc., Jim Harter (ed.). Clear wood engravings present, in extremely lifelike poses, over 1,000 species of animals. One of the most extensive pictorial sourcebooks of its kind. Captions. Index. 284pp. 9 x 12.   23766-4

CELTIC ART: The Methods of Construction, George Bain. Simple geometric techniques for making Celtic interlacements, spirals, Kells-type initials, animals, humans, etc. Over 500 illustrations. 160pp. 9 x 12. (Available in U.S. only.)   22923-8

AN ATLAS OF ANATOMY FOR ARTISTS, Fritz Schider. Most thorough reference work on art anatomy in the world. Hundreds of illustrations, including selections from works by Vesalius, Leonardo, Goya, Ingres, Michelangelo, others. 593 illustrations. 192pp. 7⅛ x 10¼.   20241-0

CELTIC HAND STROKE-BY-STROKE (Irish Half-Uncial from "The Book of Kells"): An Arthur Baker Calligraphy Manual, Arthur Baker. Complete guide to creating each letter of the alphabet in distinctive Celtic manner. Covers hand position, strokes, pens, inks, paper, more. Illustrated. 48pp. 8¼ x 11.   24336-2

EASY ORIGAMI, John Montroll. Charming collection of 32 projects (hat, cup, pelican, piano, swan, many more) specially designed for the novice origami hobbyist. Clearly illustrated easy-to-follow instructions insure that even beginning papercrafters will achieve successful results. 48pp. 8¼ x 11.   27298-2

THE COMPLETE BOOK OF BIRDHOUSE CONSTRUCTION FOR WOOD-WORKERS, Scott D. Campbell. Detailed instructions, illustrations, tables. Also data on bird habitat and instinct patterns. Bibliography. 3 tables. 63 illustrations in 15 figures. 48pp. 5¼ x 8½.   24407-5

BLOOMINGDALE'S ILLUSTRATED 1886 CATALOG: Fashions, Dry Goods and Housewares, Bloomingdale Brothers. Famed merchants' extremely rare catalog depicting about 1,700 products: clothing, housewares, firearms, dry goods, jewelry, more. Invaluable for dating, identifying vintage items. Also, copyright-free graphics for artists, designers. Co-published with Henry Ford Museum & Greenfield Village. 160pp. 8¼ x 11.   25780-0

HISTORIC COSTUME IN PICTURES, Braun & Schneider. Over 1,450 costumed figures in clearly detailed engravings–from dawn of civilization to end of 19th century. Captions. Many folk costumes. 256pp. 8⅜ x 11¾.   23150-X

LITTLE BOOK OF EARLY AMERICAN CRAFTS AND TRADES, Peter Stockham (ed.). 1807 children's book explains crafts and trades: baker, hatter, cooper, potter, and many others. 23 copperplate illustrations. 140pp. 4⅝ x 6.   23336-7

VICTORIAN FASHIONS AND COSTUMES FROM HARPER'S BAZAR, 1867–1898, Stella Blum (ed.). Day costumes, evening wear, sports clothes, shoes, hats, other accessories in over 1,000 detailed engravings. 320pp. 9⅜ x 12¼. 22990-4

GUSTAV STICKLEY, THE CRAFTSMAN, Mary Ann Smith. Superb study surveys broad scope of Stickley's achievement, especially in architecture. Design philosophy, rise and fall of the Craftsman empire, descriptions and floor plans for many Craftsman houses, more. 86 black-and-white halftones. 31 line illustrations. Introduction 208pp. 6½ x 9¼.   27210-9

THE LONG ISLAND RAIL ROAD IN EARLY PHOTOGRAPHS, Ron Ziel. Over 220 rare photos, informative text document origin (1844) and development of rail service on Long Island. Vintage views of early trains, locomotives, stations, passengers, crews, much more. Captions. 8⅞ x 11¾.   26301-0

VOYAGE OF THE LIBERDADE, Joshua Slocum. Great 19th-century mariner's thrilling, first-hand account of the wreck of his ship off South America, the 35-foot boat he built from the wreckage, and its remarkable voyage home. 128pp. 5⅜ x 8½.
40022-0

TEN BOOKS ON ARCHITECTURE, Vitruvius. The most important book ever written on architecture. Early Roman aesthetics, technology, classical orders, site selection, all other aspects. Morgan translation. 331pp. 5⅜ x 8½.   20645-9

THE HUMAN FIGURE IN MOTION, Eadweard Muybridge. More than 4,500 stopped-action photos, in action series, showing undraped men, women, children jumping, lying down, throwing, sitting, wrestling, carrying, etc. 390pp. 7⅞ x 10⅝.
20204-6 Clothbd.

TREES OF THE EASTERN AND CENTRAL UNITED STATES AND CANADA, William M. Harlow. Best one-volume guide to 140 trees. Full descriptions, woodlore, range, etc. Over 600 illustrations. Handy size. 288pp. 4½ x 6⅜.   20395-6

SONGS OF WESTERN BIRDS, Dr. Donald J. Borror. Complete song and call repertoire of 60 western species, including flycatchers, juncoes, cactus wrens, many more–includes fully illustrated booklet.   Cassette and manual 99913-0

GROWING AND USING HERBS AND SPICES, Milo Miloradovich. Versatile handbook provides all the information needed for cultivation and use of all the herbs and spices available in North America. 4 illustrations. Index. Glossary. 236pp. 5⅜ x 8½.
25058-X

BIG BOOK OF MAZES AND LABYRINTHS, Walter Shepherd. 50 mazes and labyrinths in all–classical, solid, ripple, and more–in one great volume. Perfect inexpensive puzzler for clever youngsters. Full solutions. 112pp. 8⅛ x 11.   22951-3

THE STORY OF THE TITANIC AS TOLD BY ITS SURVIVORS, Jack Winocour (ed.). What it was really like. Panic, despair, shocking inefficiency, and a little heroism. More thrilling than any fictional account. 26 illustrations. 320pp. 5⅜ x 8½. 20610-6

FAIRY AND FOLK TALES OF THE IRISH PEASANTRY, William Butler Yeats (ed.). Treasury of 64 tales from the twilight world of Celtic myth and legend: "The Soul Cages," "The Kildare Pooka," "King O'Toole and his Goose," many more. Introduction and Notes by W. B. Yeats. 352pp. 5⅜ x 8½. 26941-8

BUDDHIST MAHAYANA TEXTS, E. B. Cowell and others (eds.). Superb, accurate translations of basic documents in Mahayana Buddhism, highly important in history of religions. The Buddha-karita of Asvaghosha, Larger Sukhavativyuha, more. 448pp. 5⅜ x 8½. 25552-2

ONE TWO THREE . . . INFINITY: Facts and Speculations of Science, George Gamow. Great physicist's fascinating, readable overview of contemporary science: number theory, relativity, fourth dimension, entropy, genes, atomic structure, much more. 128 illustrations. Index. 352pp. 5⅜ x 8½. 25664-2

EXPERIMENTATION AND MEASUREMENT, W. J. Youden. Introductory manual explains laws of measurement in simple terms and offers tips for achieving accuracy and minimizing errors. Mathematics of measurement, use of instruments, experimenting with machines. 1994 edition. Foreword. Preface. Introduction. Epilogue. Selected Readings. Glossary. Index. Tables and figures. 128pp. 5⅜ x 8½. 40451-X

DALÍ ON MODERN ART: The Cuckolds of Antiquated Modern Art, Salvador Dalí. Influential painter skewers modern art and its practitioners. Outrageous evaluations of Picasso, Cézanne, Turner, more. 15 renderings of paintings discussed. 44 calligraphic decorations by Dalí. 96pp. 5⅜ x 8½. (Available in U.S. only.) 29220-7

ANTIQUE PLAYING CARDS: A Pictorial History, Henry René D'Allemagne. Over 900 elaborate, decorative images from rare playing cards (14th–20th centuries): Bacchus, death, dancing dogs, hunting scenes, royal coats of arms, players cheating, much more. 96pp. 9¼ x 12¼. 29265-7

MAKING FURNITURE MASTERPIECES: 30 Projects with Measured Drawings, Franklin H. Gottshall. Step-by-step instructions, illustrations for constructing handsome, useful pieces, among them a Sheraton desk, Chippendale chair, Spanish desk, Queen Anne table and a William and Mary dressing mirror. 224pp. 8⅛ x 11¼. 29338-6

THE FOSSIL BOOK: A Record of Prehistoric Life, Patricia V. Rich et al. Profusely illustrated definitive guide covers everything from single-celled organisms and dinosaurs to birds and mammals and the interplay between climate and man. Over 1,500 illustrations. 760pp. 7½ x 10⅛. 29371-8

Paperbound unless otherwise indicated. Available at your book dealer, online at **www.doverpublications.com**, or by writing to Dept. GI, Dover Publications, Inc., 31 East 2nd Street, Mineola, NY 11501. For current price information or for free catalogues (please indicate field of interest), write to Dover Publications or log on to **www.doverpublications.com** and see every Dover book in print. Dover publishes more than 500 books each year on science, elementary and advanced mathematics, biology, music, art, literary history, social sciences, and other areas.